SKETCHING
at the
KEYBOARD

To the memory of Emile Jacques-Dalcroze
who insisted that the sound, the feel and
the enjoyment of music must be experienced
before the use of notational symbols.

SKETCHING AT THE KEYBOARD

Harmonisation by Ear for Students of All Ages

by

LAURA CAMPBELL

Stainer & Bell, London

© 1982 Laura Campbell
First published in Great Britain by
Stainer & Bell Ltd, 82 High Road, London N2 9PW

Reprinted 1985

Campbell, Laura
    Sketching at the Keyboard
    1. Improvisation (Music)
    I. Sketching at the Keyboard
    781.6'5   MT68

ISBN 0 85249 605 2

Printed in Great Britain by Galliard (Printers) Ltd, Great Yarmouth

CONTENTS

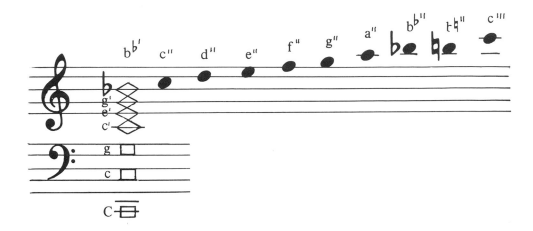

The Harmonic Series with Helmholtz identification

The Author demonstrates the method to the Incorporated Society of
Musicians: London 1981
Photograph by Susan Alcock, used with her permission

ACKNOWLEDGEMENTS

My greatest gratitude is due to Victor Whitburn, whose blind faith made possible the experimental development of this method, at first specifically for prospective teachers at St. Luke's College (now the School of Education of Exeter University) where Peter O'Brien further champions the cause by including an introductory course in the programme for the Post Graduate Certificate of Education. To Professor Ivor Keys I am profoundly indebted for his generous early support, which led to lectures and courses further afield, in this country and abroad. Also to Elizabeth Vanderspar, who invited me to teach the work, as a basis for improvisation, for the Dalcroze Teacher Training Course, now within the music department at Roehampton Institute of Higher Education, whose Chairman, Dr. Desmond Sergeant, also includes it in the syllabus for the in-service teachers' Diploma in the Teaching of Music.

Among the many whose generous encouragement helped the project I must mention John Paynter, Professor of Music, University of York, who gave precious time to reading the complete manuscript; Ann Driver; Dr. Jack Pilgrim, School of Education, University of Leeds; Eileen Craine of The British Federation of Music Festivals; and Dr. Felix Salzer, former Principal of The Mannes School of Music, New York City; also my sister Clare Campbell, of the Cambridge University Faculty of English, as a ready consultant on problems of English.

Finally, particular thanks are due to Eric Hollis, Director of the Junior Department of the London Guildhall School of Music and Drama, who gave me the opportunity to put to the test my conviction that this work is within the reach of very young children, as soon as they can play a simple melody, from notation or by ear.

Laura Campbell

Exeter,

January 1982

HOW TO USE THIS BOOK

The sequence of chapters is logically ordered in terms of the ascending harmonic series.

When the book is used for teaching small children, and beginners on the piano, this order should be adhered to and a selection of the easier examples in each chapter used. The work may begin in the very first piano lessons.

For those who have studied some harmony on paper—or who have tried other methods to harmonise at the keyboard and still need help— chapters 9 to 12 in Part II can be used in conjunction with chapters 3 to 6 in Part I. These chapters in Part II require more keyboard skill.

Part III requires some pianistic competence but, with some sacrifice of speed in performance, it is still within reach of musicians who are scarcely pianists, for the purpose of making arrangements for groups of instruments.

The Appendix contains notes intended for teachers and some 'answers', but do not look at them in advance!

INTRODUCTION

First the appetite, then the culture
(Arthur Hutchings)

The teaching of harmony has probably remained less influenced by contemporary knowledge of how people think and learn than any other subject.

The case for teaching harmony at the keyboard before, and then alongside written harmony ought not still to need vindicating. If keyboard harmony is required in higher musical education, as is now almost universally the case, it is even more necessary as the starting point for teaching harmony in schools. Only when the standard in practical harmony amongst upper school music specialists is raised can a better standard amongst average entrants to higher education be expected. Unfortunately in most schools harmony is still carried out only on paper, the aim being that what is written should be heard in the head. But what most often goes on in the head is 'A root, a 3rd, a 5th, and double the..., but then this can't follow that, because...etc.'. Is it surprising if the result sounds as purposeless as the words of a crossword puzzle read consecutively, when the method used *is* equivalent to that of a crossword puzzle?

It is probable that few teachers realise how much is *not* heard in the head (even by many musical pupils) and that, to most, harmony is a foreign language—the logic of whose sentences is not understood though individual words can often be spelled out. Little wonder, when the teaching processes are akin to the sterile pastime of 'Painting by Numbers', in which numbered areas on a printed drawing are to be filled in by colours specified on an accompanying chart. Such an educationally shallow method would not be accepted by responsible teachers of art or languages today. In language teaching, the approach is increasingly to develop hearing and speaking before writing, on the grounds that this is how one learns a mother tongue. In music, this approach means recognising that sounds must be heard in the head before they can be reproduced to mean something intended. It means working from sound to symbol, not symbol to sound; and from the known to the unknown. Given a familiar melody, in which he has some idea of what he wants to hear, the student will find that a chord which theoretically will 'fit' may or may not produce the harmonisation he expects to hear in the particular context. He is then able to search for his own correction by reference to that pattern in his expectant ear and enjoy the satisfaction of discovering the wanted sound. Having linked a wanted sound with a way of producing it, through his own discovery—which is quite different from being told or shown it—he is more likely to remember the association. In this way he is learning to sense what *may* apply to similar situations in unfamiliar melodies.

Only the instinctive improviser, knowing how a passage should sound, automatically knows what to do to produce those sounds. Aural recognition and analytical labelling are not synonymous. One cannot teach an instinct—only demonstrate what it achieves. Instinct by-passes conscious thought. For the majority of students the need is *not* to be shown what to do but to be taught how to *think* in order to discover for themselves what to do.

This method should be taught with virtually no demonstration. The role of the teacher is to prod the student in the right direction by asking the kind of questions he needs to learn to ask himself. All the playing is done by the students: and improvements stem from their own, their colleagues' and teacher's comments and comparisons. Students learn as much from critical listening to each others' performances as from their own. The work is essentially a process of aural training. Traditional teaching of harmony has too often been detached not only from aural training and extemporisation but also from history, form and analysis, orchestration and composition (even tending to be detrimental to original composition).

Music, to be such, must move. It must progress horizontally in time. The traditional system of working out chords by a vertical process of construction is a contradiction in terms when it comes to practical music making. Nor is that process the way in which music evolved. It brings the student in too late historically, aurally, mentally and manually.

The creative process in any art form involves gradual emergence, at first in the form of a sketch. We tend to think of a sketch as being essentially a 'rough' draft, something imprecise and therefore inapplicable to music, where precision of rhythmic duration and still more of pitch are vital. But a sketch need not necessarily be imprecise. It may take the form of an outline, which is *precise as far as it goes*.

That is the basis of approach in this book. Sketching at the keyboard—and the method can be applied with advantage to written harmony, too—is a process akin to dressing a cut-out cardboard doll, whom we may call 'Melody', first in basic underwear then in a choice of costumes of varying degree of elaboration which need to be selected to suit the wearer and a given occasion.

These sketching techniques provide, in a systematic order, corresponding layers of 'dressing' for a tune, any one of which may be selected either as an end-product or as a foundation for further embellishment. At the same time, the simplest processes musically are also those which make the simplest demands on the student, both as thinker and as executant. This enables him to produce a *complete piece at every stage of study*. Only so can one learn the relationship of harmony to rhythm and to form, which is rhythm on a large scale. Every pupil has as much right to expect the satisfaction of producing complete pieces in harmony as in instrumental lessons. This is vital to motivation, without which little work of enduring value will be done.

Playing by ear by-passes notation; so as little notation as possible is used in this book, in which the method of working is based on (i) listening and (ii) reasoning. Visual preoccupation detracts from aural attention. The skilled improviser does not think in terms of individual notes, but of ideas, involving processes. In ordinary notation, where all note-heads look alike, such processes are not apparent; so when notation is used here, different patterns of note-head are used to clarify them.

The simplicity of the instrumental technique needed at the outset makes it possible to start this course as soon as a pupil can play a simple melody on the piano. This means that music students whose first instrument may be string, wind or voice, and who may be only beginners at the piano, have no need to feel as disadvantaged as they so often do in a practical harmony course.

It is generally accepted that the mind can only cope with one thing at a time in the *foreground* of consciousness. Other simultaneous concerns recede in stages as they become what we call 'taken for granted', eventually perhaps producing an automatic reaction. So the truly educational teaching of skills depends on intelligent presentation of material in the *order* in which it can usefully take precedence in the foreground of mental and physical consciousness. A series of problems demanding attention must proceed consecutively, that is, horizontally in the dimension of time.

The present process teaches the student to think in terms of *single ideas to cover whole stretches of material*. As knowledge and physical competence advance, the substance can become richer vertically as groups of sounds, chords and chord sequences are grasped as single units, their components being taken for granted by mind and fingers. Students are encouraged to 'see the wood for the trees', avoiding bad elaboration in favour of good simplicity; so that good elaboration, in a variety of styles, may follow.

The method is in no way a gimmick, nor does it rest on an arbitrary selection of processes. It is scientifically based on a systematic use of the harmonic series. This involves real understanding, through the ear, of the acoustic reasons for rules formerly learned as arbitrary dicta for application on paper. It also advantageously alters the order in which aspects of harmony may be taught, bringing in earlier certain important musical features traditionally considered advanced.

From their very first term of work students—and indeed school children—can provide their own simple piano accompaniments for singing suitable songs. Being able to put the skill to practical use in this way provides for the player the kind of pleasure and incentive that is needed to lift the Cinderella of old 'Harmony' out of her drabness and chores and take her dancing to the ball.

First 'stimulate the appetite'; then the culture of extemporisation which flourished in earlier times may be revived with an enthusiasm long overdue.

PART I

1 START WITH A SHAPE

You may be a competent pianist with a repertoire of Beethoven, Chopin and Mozart, or you may be a virtual beginner who can do little more than play a simple melody on the piano. If you were suddenly asked to play for 'Musical Chairs' at a childrens' party would you be able to? This is the least that is generally expected of anyone with pretensions to playing a musical instrument.

It is preferable for a group of players, however mixed their ability, to do this first task together, as their contributions are likely to be very contrasted and much can be learnt from comparison. What is important is not who is the best pianist, but who can play something suitable for the occasion. So a single line of melody, suitable in tempo and touch to the movements of a child will prove more apt than the slow movement of a classical sonata or a piece of improvised jazz which the player is unable to vary as the game progresses.

Don't look for printed music. Have the courage to sit down at the piano and 'have a go' at doing this—right now! If you find it difficult at present, you will not do so by the end of this chapter: and by the end of chapter 3 you should be able to make a good showing at an actual children's party, playing accompanied melodies for walking, running and skipping, by ear.

This first exercise may serve as an audition for a group of new students in their first class of keyboard harmony, enabling the teacher to sub-group them according to the ability revealed, which may present quite a different picture from 'examination qualifications'.

When all have had a chance to show their paces, it may transpire that a string or wind player who knows he cannot do more on the piano than play the melody of a simple folk tune or nursery rhyme makes one of the more appropriate contributions. This provides the launching pad for the next task, from which even the most competent may learn something, if only the importance of extending the conception of 'harmony' to include some essential ingredients of composition and orchestration.

The First Steps

1 Three Blind Mice or Frère Jacques

(i)   Play the melody of 'Three Blind Mice' by ear, or 'Frère Jacques', if you want an easier melody. To do this, first play a keynote (*c'* or, preferably, *d'*) and think which degree of the chosen scale the melody starts on: 1st, 2nd, 3rd, 4th or what?

(ii)   Here you have a single line of melody, which runs along *horizontally* in the medium of time. What would be the simplest, and historically the earliest, way of providing *vertical* enrichment for a line of melody?

Imagine a primitive village community having a sing-song round a camp fire. What would happen when the women and children are joined by the men, with everyone singing the same tune?

Play the tune again, adding what the men would sing with your left hand. Notice how playing in octaves like this strengthens the melody and immediately gives it the conviction of being 'a piece': one that could suitably be played for children to march or skip to. Such a version would indeed sound more professional than an imperfect chordal harmonisation.

(iii)   A feature of this piece is repetition. In nature there are a myriad leaves on a myriad trees, a myriad pebbles on a myriad beaches. But works of art are the result of intentional design, and repetition needs to convince the listener that it is intended; otherwise a musical repetition may sound like a record player on which the needle has got stuck in a groove.

Such conviction may be achieved by altering the manner in which a phrase is played when repeated. What do you think would be the simplest way of differentiating between a phrase and its repeat? Play the whole piece on this principle, with left hand still doubling the right-hand melody line an octave below.

Never think that when you are doing 'harmony', dynamics (variations of loud and soft tone) do not matter. Dynamics are an essential element of musical composition and the choice of them may influence the choice and arrangement of harmonies. Changing dynamics is the simplest way of differentiating between statement and repeat of a phrase.

(iv)   Now it happens that the octave, which is the natural distance at which men and women will sing the same tune, is also the first interval in what is known as the **Harmonic Series**. Pythagoras discovered this basic principle in the physics of sound when, in ancient Greece, his experiments led him to 'stop' a stretched string midway and he found that plucking either half produced the 'same' sound an octave higher than that produced by the full length.

The frontispiece (p. vi) demonstrates the harmonic series, the lowest note of which is known as the 'Fundamental' and generates the sounds above. The next sound, an octave (8ve) above, is called the first 'overtone' or 'upper partial', as part of the total vibrating object will also be producing that sound, more softly.

You can hear this at the piano by depressing the sustaining pedal (the right pedal, which removes the dampers from the strings, so leaving them free to vibrate 'in sympathy' with related sounds) and striking any low note loudly, with your left hand, as though you were striking a gong (most effectively done with the little finger side of the hand, thumb uppermost). Then with your right hand play, very softly, every other note of the same letter name, ascending to the top of the piano. You will find that these notes sound as though they were already 'partially' there. Another way is to press down a note in the centre of the keyboard so slowly that it does not sound at all. This is simply to remove its damper. Keep that key depressed and strike—short and sharp—the note an octave below. What happens?

Musicians say these sounds that are so alike, yet not identical, are the same sound at a different pitch, or in a different 'register'. **Registration** is a very important tool in composition, orchestration and improvisation. On the piano you have a large range of registers available. Think of them as though you were handling an orchestra.

(v)   Play the tune again, but this time differentiate between statement and repeat of phrases by means of change of register. In other words, play repeat phrases up or down one or more octaves. Consider how you may reinforce your previous choices of dynamic contrast by the added resource of registration: how you can pair the musical elements of loud/soft with those of high/low; or simply substitute the musical 'colour' of registration for that of dynamics.

Haphazard use of different registers will be found to confuse rather than clarify the structure of a piece. You need to find patterns which emphasise the phrase relationships to bring the shape of the piece, the **Form** of it, into 'relief', as sculptors say when figures carved on the pediment of a temple or on a modern building are made to stand out from each other and from their background.

After the two paired phrases in 'Three Blind Mice', how many different ways can you find to highlight the *threesome* structure of the third phrase by means of registration?

Ex. 1

Where?   Where?

Where?   Where?

Suggestions are given in the Appendix (page 231), but you will spoil your fun if you look before making your own discoveries with each song. So when you look at suggestions there, *do not look ahead*.

(vi) Play 'Frère Jacques' over itself. Start with the right hand on *c″* and bring in the left hand with the same tune starting on *c* at "dormez vous". Then start with the left hand and bring the right hand in *one* 8ve above.

2 Come Home Now

German

Come home   now, come home   now, The bask - et's full,   the

work   is   done;   Come home   now, come home   now, Our

work   to - day   is   done.____ We've   earned   our sup - per,

you'll a - gree, And   we're   as   hung - ry   as   can be; Come

home   now, come home now, Our work to - day   is   done.

Reprinted by permission of Oxford University Press.

16

The next task is to treat an unfamiliar melody by registration, in order to bring the form of the piece into relief and, at the same time, make an interesting arrangement of it such as could be transferred to a group of solo instruments. Always be alert to the importance of words in a song, both to their meaning and to the breathing natural to putting them across. Repeated remarks, verbal or musical, should convince that they are intentional, not mechanical reiteration. Before starting on 'Come Home Now', compare music and words of the first section with this:

Ex. 2   *18th century English*

My   grand-sire beat the   drum com-plete, His   name was Dar - by   Kel - ly   O!

(i)   After you have decided the phrasing of 'Come Home Now', set the song using the vocabulary of processes introduced so far, which include:

    (a)   Unison, at any pitch
    (b)   Octave doubling, at any distance
    (c)   Changes of registration of either, to bring the formal pattern of phrase structure into relief.

If you find problems, consider that in 'Three Blind Mice' the passage that required threefold treatment consisted of repetitions, all of equal length. This song presents a new threefold situation, that of phrases which are short, short, long. If you associate the concepts of short/long with light/strong, you may find a satisfying solution in terms of orchestration on the piano. Consider carefully the registers you use.

The middle section, bars 9–12, is only slightly contrasted; but the 'recapitulation' (repeat of the first section) makes it desirable to emphasise contrast here. Find a way of making this section stand out from the rest.

When you have completed your arrangement, see if you can play the whole from memory. If this proves easier than expected, recognise that the way you were thinking made it easier than trying to remember each note individually.

Most of the processes used in this book aim at assembling musical phenomena into groups which, as they become familiar mentally and manually, can be conceived and played as *units* of some length. For this is how the proficient improviser works, consciously or sub-consciously: he does not give a separate thought to each component note or chord. When you have completed your arrangement of 'Come Home Now' compare it, in terms of registration, with the Appendix (page 231).

(ii)   These simple pieces introduce basic considerations concerning the nature and justification of repetition. After a first hearing of material one may need the reminder and emphasis of repetition. But when, after a diversion or development of that original (equivalent to a discussion of it) the first statement reappears, further repetition is superfluous. Compare the shapes of 'Frère Jacques' and 'Three Blind Mice'.

3 The Animals Went In

To musicians, form in music has an abstract drama of its own. Additionally, registration is extremely useful as a means of highlighting the realistic drama of programmatic ideas and words. As an example, consider the words of various verses of this song. Play the melody, solo or doubled as you wish, and choose a suitable register (or ask your youngest relative to do so!) for line 6 of the third and final verses.

18

The Use of Octaves by Composers

Students are inclined to confuse issues of *ease* and *difficulty* with value judgements, owing to the emphasis placed in training on learning to do increasingly difficult things. Composers of integrity do not think in that way. What is good is whatever expresses what the composer wants to convey: not an abstract 'right', but the right thing in the right place, namely *relevance to context*. So what is 'clever' may sometimes be so simple that it never occurred to those with more ambition than imagination!

Here are two examples of Beethoven's frequent use of octave texture:

Ex. 3   *Opening of Piano Sonata, Op. 2, No. 2*

Opening of the Slow Movement, Piano Concerto No. 4, Op. 28

The orchestra plays solely in octaves right up to the last few bars of the

19

movement, creating a texture in striking contrast with the harmonies of the piano.

Once you have used octaves, and your mind and ear are alerted to them, you will begin to recognise octave passages and changes of register surprisingly frequently in musical performances. Make your own collection of examples.

4 Hot Cross Buns

There is another ingenious way in which composers make use of the octave concept. Though this is usually regarded as the province of advanced musical study, any beginner can be introduced to the technique quite simply with 'Hot Cross Buns'. The words alone should serve as a reminder of the tune:

> Hot Cross Buns
> (*repeat*)
>
> One a penny, two a penny
> (*recapitulate phrase 1*)

(i)   Sing the melody and decide which degree of the scale it starts on.

(ii)   Play the melody with the right hand, in the key of G.

(iii)   Double the melody at the octave with the left hand.

(iv)   Play both hands together again, but this time play each phrase of the left hand melody upside down, as a mirror image, in contrary motion to the right hand. Choose a suitable register, so that both parts sound clearly.

This musical technique is known as **inversion**. It needs to be used with musical intelligence rather than mathematical precision. You are probably already aware of this device of inversion in the visual arts: in the printing of wallpapers and textiles the block containing the basic engraved pattern may also be used in reverse, to enrich the overall design. If you find any problem with this piece, bear this in mind and simply reverse the bar concerned. The Appendix (page 232) explains what you have probably discovered for yourself.

(v)   Take particular note of the first phrase of this song, played right way up by the left hand, as this makes a very useful bass unit for phrase endings. Notice that it consists of the 5th degree of any key, subsequently dropped an octave, followed by the keynote: 5-5-1.

20

There is no need to delay the use of this bass until it is associated with three chords in four parts. In the meantime, it will be referred to as the 'Hot Cross Buns' bass (**'HXB'**). From now on, listen for it, and also for the use of octaves, in all the music you hear, piano *or* orchestral.

(vi)   Play 'Three Blind Mice' over 'HXB' *under each phrase*.

Further Songs

Stick to the restriction of using only the processes introduced in this chapter, namely:

(a)   Solo
(b)   Doubling (at the distance of one or more octaves)
(c)   Change of register
(d)   Inversion (very occasionally)

Discover what can be done within these limitations. In the long run, this is the way to develop a variety of styles. People who are competent at harmonising hymn tunes often tend to play everything as though it were a hymn!

In the following songs the prime reason for decisions may be dramatic; but try also to see how your choices may make a musically pleasing result as well.

Fire Down Below

English Sea Shanty

Captain Morgan's March

Here is an excellent opportunity for the use of inversion. The sections may be labelled as *Verse* 'A,B,A,B' and *Chorus* with its repeat 'C,C'. In which section is inversion most effective? End the repeat of the chorus with bass 'HXB'. See Appendix (page 232).

Down in Demerera

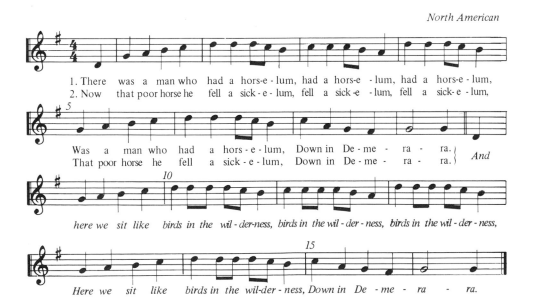

First double the tune at the octave. Then invert the bass.

22

Camptown Races

Stephen Foster

The Camp-town la-dies sing this song, Doo-dah! doo-dah! The

Camp-town race-track five miles long, Oh! doo-dah day! I

come down there wid my hat caved in, Doo-dah!__ doo-dah!__ I

go back home wid a poc-ket full of tin, Oh! doo-dah day!

Gwine to run all night! Gwine to run all day! I'll__

bet my mon-ey on the bob-tail nag, Some-bo-dy bet on the bay.

2 SET STYLE AND PACE

In Chapter 1, the earliest *vocal* music was considered: that of men and women singing the same melody together at the distance of an octave, the first interval in the harmonic series. Later in the chapter, octaves and the derived concept of registration were used to highlight the form of a piece of music. Next in order of importance is to decide **Style** and **Pace**. To consider these it is helpful to turn to the earliest *instrumental* music.

1 Papa a du Tabac

Imagine a strolling peasant musician in the late Middle Ages, wandering from one local fairground to another on foot, playing a melody such as this old French folk tune, later known as 'Papa a du Tabac'. What instruments do you think might have been used for its performance? The most primitive instruments (as also in a sophisticated modern orchestra) involve banging, blowing, bowing and plucking. Our mediaeval fairground musician would probably have played this tune on the pipe and tabor. The tabor was a little drum held at the hip by a cord slung over the opposite shoulder and beaten with one hand, leaving the other free to play the small pipe. So the one player could play two instruments at the same time. You can imitate this combination on the piano, with a little imagination.

(i)   What drum rhythm do you think would be suitable for this tune? Tap whatever rhythm comes to you, with the flat of your left hand on your left thigh. It should be a simple rhythmic pattern, not a mere

24

repeated beat. Rhythm is more a matter of physical feeling than intellectual thought; so don't think in terms of notation, but let the rhythm come naturally through your hand, while you sing the melody.

(ii)   Transfer this drum rhythm to the piano keys with the left hand. Make use of the *second interval in the harmonic series, the 5th.* (See frontispiece, p. vi.) The melody is in the key of C, so the 5th used will be that from a bass *c* to *g* above it. Another name for the keynote is the 'Tonic', so this interval will be called the **Tonic 5th** (to signify *both notes*, the keynote with the 5th above it). Finger it with little finger on *c* and thumb on *g*. This distance will soon become a single feeling for your hand, so that you do not have to think of two notes. Touch and balance of tone are vital to style. When playing this 5th to imitate a drum, use a crisp, light, dry *staccato* touch, from the wrist, keeping the forearm still. This is best practised on the closed lid of the piano to secure the right sharp, vibrant, percussive tone.

(iii)   Start with a few bars of introduction. Then bring in the melody, at first sung, then played, and see that the bass does not drown it. Compare the effect of putting the Tonic 5th interval into different registers beneath the melody. Which register makes it sound most like a drum?

(iv)   Some may prefer the closer register, some an octave lower; each for good reasons. It will be seen from the frontispiece (page vi) that the harmonic series carries a complete scale in the fourth octave above the fundamental. The interval of a fifth (*c–g*) is two octaves below the scale. To show that relationship (8ve lower than the frontispiece), stop on the first note of each bar and listen to the effect:

Ex. 4

etc.

The wide distance between melody and bass separates the bass from the melody, giving the bass almost no pitch significance. Its only pitch function is to define the key. Otherwise its contribution is entirely *rhythmic* (so you must feel it, *not* write it down).

25

Now listen to the first bar with the bass played in the close register:

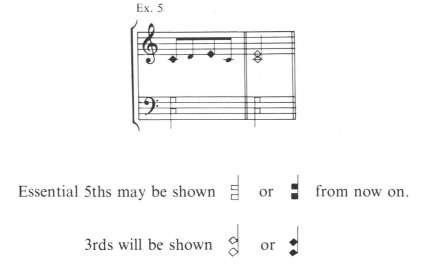

Ex. 5.

Essential 5ths may be shown ⬧ or ⬧ from now on.

3rds will be shown ⬧ or ⬧

You may prefer this as the 'more musical' sound, for you will hear that the combination is acoustically perfectly blended. Comparison with the frontispiece reveals that this is exactly the arrangement in which the main component notes of any chord first occur, in terms of the physics of sound. In this close register the *pitch* significance of the bass is stronger—for better in some bars, for worse in others. The distant register sounds more detached from the melody. So it is more effective to suggest a drum accompaniment.

(v)   However, once the suggestion of imitating pipe and tabor in this way has been established in the first line, use the wider resources of the piano to make a more interesting piece. Now highlight the overall **Form** of the piece by means of registration, as you did in the previous chapter. You can change the register of the melody or the bass, or both. In the last four bars of the melody, can you indicate through registration that, this time, these bars are not going to be repeated, as the piece is drawing to a close?

Add a rhythmic 'Postlude' to balance the Introduction or 'Prelude' you provided. This will complete the effect of dying away. *After* completion, compare with the Appendix (page 233).

(vi)   Play the whole in another key, in F sharp or B. You will only have to find the Tonic 5th of the key and then concentrate on the melody.

(vii)   Here is another setting of the first part of this piece:

26

Ex. 6

Which arrangement do you consider more appropriate to the melody, this or the setting with accompaniment of Tonic 5ths in a rhythmic motif?

By making rhythmic use of the interval of a Tonic 5th throughout, the **Style** of the piece and its **Pace** have been established. For style and pace hang together. In the case of many pieces, this particular sketch process may clearly reveal *where* you want to place the harmonies (and subsequently their textural arrangement) when you come to deciding them. For *where* is a prior consideration to *what*.

Just as an oil painting is not innately superior to a watercolour or a line drawing, a less colourful musical process may prove an ideal ultimate style for a particular piece, or section of a piece. In this piece it is generally agreed that the simple 'drone bass' treatment is more suitable stylistically than the close texture of example 6. Aesthetic value rests upon stylistic aptness, not upon considerations of ease and difficulty. It belongs to the permanent and adult world of any art: whereas value scales of 'elementary' and 'advanced' are only educational concerns. To be a preparation for that adult world, aesthetic education is at least as important as technical training. The drawings of great cartoonists, as well as the sketches of great painters, show how a skilful outline can indicate a total structure. (Try to look at reproductions of drawings by Leonardo da Vinci and James Thurber.)

(viii) **Pace** and **Speed** are not quite the same thing, though they interact. Pace is concerned with the inter-relationship between different levels of a musical texture, between melody and accompaniment. The rhythmic pattern or 'motif' usually chosen for the bass 5ths here is 'slow: quick, quick'. This can, of course, be written in any of the following ways:

Rhythmic notation is arbitrarily chosen by composers, because, unlike pitch notation, it is only relative (within a context) and not associated with any fixed scale of durational measurements. None of the above notations define any speed. But apply 'slow: quick, quick' to 'Papa a du Tabac' in these three *proportions*, in terms of the melody as it is written, and observe what effect each has on the total structure. You will then understand what **Pace** means, and be able to answer:

    (a)   Which makes the melody go the fastest?
    (b)   Which makes the melody go the slowest?
    (c)   Which seems to you the most natural?

If you were making a set of variations on such a tune, you might well use all three. For example, you might make it race along by making more of the melody pass between one supporting throb and another (equivalent to a high gear). Such treatment could make an exciting *coda* or *finale*. Another pace may destroy the vivacity of the melody, weighing it down to a lugubrious plod, but could yet prove appropriate as a slow processional variation in the style of a funeral march. This might lead you to vary the melody changing the tonality to minor:

Ex. 7

Slow

etc.

Such a train of thought may indicate why slow movements of classical sonatas and symphonies are written in such fast *looking* notes: because what might be called the structural pace (as opposed to the ticking beats) moves so slowly there is room for a lot of musical 'conversation' between one main underlying pulse and the next.

    There may, therefore, be alternative suitable paces for one melody, according to the occasion of its performance and the nature of its arrangement. What is unfortunately true is that the habit of arranging folk songs and dances (such as many carols) in a continuous 4-part texture for SATB (soprano, alto, tenor, bass) frequently leads to the destruction of the rhythmic character and flow of the original melody. However you mean to arrange a melody in the long run, it is well to start by appreciating its virgin qualities: rhythm, inflection and natural pace.

2 Patapan

French Carol

Wil - lie, take your lit - tle drum, With your whis - tle, Ro - bin, come! When we hear the fife and drum, *Tu - re - lu - re - lu,* *pat - a - pat - a - pan,* When we hear the fife and drum, Christ-mas should be___ fro - lic - some.

The aptness of a 5ths rhythmic bass to this carol is obvious.

(i)   Play the melody, which, whether you can put a name to the tonality or not, will enable you to hear the right 5th to apply throughout.

(ii)   There are two alternative ways of fitting the same rhythm to this melody, so establishing two different paces. Can you play both? One clue is to be found in speaking the words in their natural rhythm. Which do you prefer? Where would you start the rhythmic accompaniment, in each case? What effect does each pace of combining melody and accompaniment have on the speed of the carol? Maybe, both could be combined; the slower on a pitched 5th (piano or other suitable instrument) and the faster on a light drum? See the Appendix (page 233).

3 Skip to my Lou

Find a rhythmic accompaniment that establishes the right pace for this melody, using Tonic 5ths only. When you have reached your conclusion, compare it with the series of sketches in the Appendix (page 233).

4 This Old Man

Make a rhythmic accompaniment throughout this song, using Tonic 5th only. Play the 5th no more than twice in each bar.

Where is the most important place to play it? Where is the next most important place?

The resulting figure is one of the most useful rhythms, for many speeds of tune, owing to its capacity to propel the music onwards over the bar line. See the Appendix (page 234).

5 Marching through Georgia

North American

Bring the good old bu - gle, boys, we'll sing an - oth - er song,

Sing it with a spi - rit that will start the world a - long,

Sing it as we used to sing it fif - ty thou -sand strong,

While we were march - ing through Geor - gia. Hur -

rah! hur - rah! we bring the Jub - i - lee! Hur -

rah! hur - rah! the flag that makes you free!

So we sang the cho - rus from At - lan - ta to the sea,

While we were march - ing through Geor - gia!

Sometimes, however, a rhythmic *pattern* is not what is wanted. The obvious rhythmic basis of a tune such as this is a 'left, right' march round the room.

(i) Do this, while you sing the tune.

(ii) Play the same vivacious 'left, right' with your two hands on the closed lid of the piano, singing the tune.

(iii) Open the lid and play the same 'left, right' with a vivacious staccato touch on Tonic 5ths in two registers (both *below* the melody) while you, or others, sing the tune.

Registration has been used here for a rhythmic purpose, to highlight the 'down' and 'up' of strong and weak beats.

Small children can enjoy playing these 5ths and acting as 'conductor' at the piano, showing with facial expression, head and shoulders where the singers should sing loudly or softly.

Further Variations of Rhythmic Pattern and Touch Quality

'Drone basses', as these exclusively Tonic accompaniments are called, do not always need to imitate staccato percussive rhythms, but may be a sustained legato when this suits the context. The following songs provide scope for a variety of touches and rhythmic patterns. They may be taken in any order.

6 Spring Song (Frühlingslied)

Far from being naïve, treatment by Tonic 5th would probably have been the basis of the style in which a German lieder writer might have arranged this song. See the Appendix, page 234, for one possibility.

7 Turn the Glasses Over

North American

I've been to Har-lem, I've been to Do - ver, I've tra -velled this wide world, all o - ver, O - ver, o - ver, three times o - ver, Drink what you have to drink and turn the glas-ses o - ver. Sail - ing east, sail - ing west, Sail - ing o - ver the o - cean, Bet-ter watch out when the boat be - gins to rock, Or you'll lose your girl in the o - cean.

Try using left hand once and right hand twice in each bar for this roistering sea song, while you sing the melody. On what beats will you play the right hand?

8 Jim along Josie

American

So busy a melody requires only simple rhythmic support. Interest can be added by adventurous registration.

9 Cockles and Mussels

This song in triple time is no smooth flowing waltz, but a ballad of the poor struggling girl, stumbling up the cobbled streets with her barrow. Can you indicate this in musical terms? At what point in the first bar does the singer need support? In the second bar? Then where there are equal crotchets in the melody what could you do? Notice the interesting rhythmic counterpoint that you are producing.

10 The British Grenadiers

19th century English

Some talk of Al - ex - an - der, And some of Her - cu - les, Of
Hec-tor and Ly - san - der, And such great names as

these; But of all the world's brave he - - roes There's none that can com - pare With a

tow, row, row, row, row, row, row, For the Brit-ish Gre - na - diers.

(i) Do you find any objection to alternating registers with the left hand 5th beneath the melody, at a suitable pace for the song?

(ii) Now play the 5th on the opposite pair of beats, the off-beats, very short and crisp and in one register only. Play 5ths again, beating time (at two minims to the bar) with your right hand, while you sing the melody.

The Appendix (page 234) concerns songs 6 to 10: consult it on completion of all five.

Use of the 'Tonic Pedal' by Composers

Composers frequently build prolonged passages, or even a complete variation in a set of variations, on a Tonic bass, known as a 'Tonic Pedal' (a term derived from the playing of such bass notes on an organ pedal). Examples include the 8th and 22nd of Brahms's *Variations on a Theme of Handel* and, from Mendelssohn's '*Variations Sérieuses*', no. 11 and the following (no. 5):

Ex. 8
Agitato

Play this variation reduced to a single-line melody over a Tonic 5th throughout, making it easier to read it at the correct pace and *agitato:*

Ex. 9
Agitato

(or 8ve lower)

Studying the works of the great composers will reveal what good use may be made of the simplest concepts: never regard them as 'outgrown'.

3 HARMONIC LANDSCAPING: I

1 Girls and Boys Come Out to Play

> Girls and boys come out to play
> The moon doth shine as bright as day,
> Leave your supper and leave your sleep
> And come with your playfellows into the street.
>
> Come with a whoop and come with a call,
> Come with a good will or not at all.
> Up the ladder and down the wall,
> A penny loaf will serve you all.

The words will serve to remind you of the tune, so that you can play it by ear.

(i)   Sing the melody of the first verse and, without touching the piano, decide which degree of the scale it starts on.

(ii)   Play the melody of the first verse, in the key of G.

(iii)   Accompany it according to the previous chapter, with left hand Tonic 5ths at appropriate rhythmic points.

(iv)   If this seems rather heavy and stodgy, you may either be playing the 5th too frequently, or you may not be considering registration. Beat two with your left hand 'Down, up: Down, up'. Then interpret this 'Down, up' in terms of registration on the keyboard, with your left hand, to highlight the 'Strong, light' of the metric pulse. That should set it dancing! Indeed, this simple setting would be ideal to fulfil the challenge of Chapter 1 to extemporise for 'Musical Chairs' at a children's party.

(v)   What happens to the melody in the second verse? (If you do not know the whole tune, turn to the Appendix (page 235) for the second verse.) Is it identical? In what way does it differ? Play the second verse and accompany it with the appropriate 5th.

   You may either consider the first verse to be in the key of G, accompanied by its Tonic 5th and the second verse to be in the key of D with its Tonic 5th; or you may regard the first verse as needing the Tonic chord of G and the second verse as needing the chord on the fifth degree of the scale of G, called the 'Dominant'. Dominant chord or in the key of the Dominant—it does not matter in this case.

What *is* important is to realise that you can hear an alternative chord by the same process as you recognise the major or minor tonality of a whole melody, through listening to the melodic *line*. Do not *look* at each separate note and calculate chords that might be deemed to 'fit'. Working that way will not tend to make musical sense.

The accepted definition of harmony as being the 'simultaneous combination' of sounds of different pitch is misleading. For harmony is not exclusively vertical, and may equally be implied by a *horizontal progression of sounds*, by melody, as you have already discovered. (See the Appendix, page 232.) So we proceed by looking at the whole ground to be covered—that is, the whole of a melody—and by **'Harmonic Landscaping'**.

If you visit a nursery garden or bulb field, it is easy to distinguish between large patches of one flower and another. It needs much more knowledge and skill to take one look at a herbaceous border and be able to recognise, remember and name each flower in the rich mixture. Harmonic landscaping involves viewing a piece of music as one might view an area of land from the air—the proverbial bird's eye view—and establishing essential outlines, as a painter might make a charcoal sketch prior to an oil painting. Details, in both art forms, logically come later. To embark on harmonisation with the idea that it consists of planting one little lump of sound after another, like rods in a park railing, is to be led down the garden path!

2 Michael Finnigin

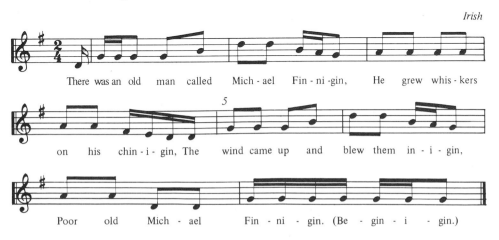

In 'Girls and boys come out to play' one entire section of the piece was covered by Tonic harmony, the sequential repeat by Dominant harmony. In this song:

(i)   What are the areas to be covered by Tonic 5th and Dominant 5th?

(ii)   There is a tradition with several nonsense songs such as this that each succeeding verse is performed in a key one semitone higher; each final keynote, on 'Beg-in-i-gin', being regarded as leading to the next key, so:

The note G is the seventh degree of the scale of A♭: this degree is called the 'leading note' (that is, leading to the tonic). At the end of *this* verse you need to think of A♭ as G♯, leading note (seventh degree) of the key of A. This is good practice for gaining facility in playing Tonic and Dominant 5th in all keys. Notice that the overlap involved in dropping to the Dominant 5th links two chords together aurally and manually:

The Mis-use of 'Closed' Positions

Amongst any group of people following this course there are always

39

some who think they can improve upon open bass 5th by using the full chord. Compare:

Ex. 11a

Ex. 11b

Careful listening will reveal that, far from being an improvement, the latter is indefensible; whereas the slight discord on beat 2 of bar 1 in the 5ths version adds a frosty nip to the moonlight escapade. The former can enable a child to sound like a professional: the latter can make a professional sound like an amateur.

Generations of students have been led to think that the basis of harmony is a clutch of sounds like this:

Consequently many people who would like to play by ear set about it like this:

Ex. 12a   *Improvisation*

etc.

40

Ex. 12b   *Harmonisation*

etc.

Would you agree that those clutches of sound in the left hand have obscured rather than highlighted the melody? They have weighed it down, destroyed its lightness and bounce, its *joie de vivre*. No wonder such attempts lead to discouragement, especially amongst the more musically sensitive. Further, such a texture cannot lead to improvement, because the muddy quality of sound prevents players from hearing clearly what they are doing. It is only through careful listening to a texture of transparent clarity that the ear can play its essential critical role. As with watercolour painting, it is easier to add than to take away. The harmonic series (p. vi) now reveals that these three notes known as a 'triad' only occur *next to each other* (in what is called 'close position') within the *third* octave of the series, not in what is generally regarded as the accompanying area of the keyboard (for practical purposes the province of the left hand). In the accompanying area (the *second* octave span above the 'fundamental' lowest note) there is only a 5th. That 5th alone *implies a chord*, as it sets into vibration the overtones capable of defining it further.

Regard the fundamental itself simply as lower 8ve doubling of a bass note. Then the three notes which *define a chord* first occur positioned like this:

Ex. 12c

You will notice that this arrangement produces a total sound of the utmost clarity, because it is perfectly blended acoustically. It involves placing the 3rd of the triad a 10th above the root, never in between the root and the 5th in a low register...unless you really want, for

41

some specific dramatic purpose, a thick and heavy sound. Beethoven obviously did want such a sound in:

Ex. 12d *Adagio ma non troppo*

In 'Girls and boys' and 'Michael Finnigin' the melody (right hand area for the pianist) clearly delineates the harmony in terms of the close-position triad, while the bass 5th clinches it beneath:

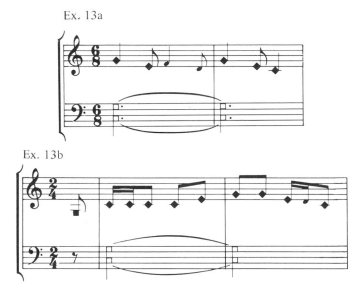

Ex. 13a

Ex. 13b

The reason why placing the 3rd of a triad at a low pitch, in between the root and its 5th, causes an ugly sound as in Ex. 12, may now be understood. This is especially so on a modern piano, because of its 're-sonance'. For this 3rd in the low register will set up its own harmonic series, evoking the following admixture of overtones:

A chord played like this:  produces overtones like this:

Ex. 14a

Ex. 14a(i)

It is this simultaneous evocation of $b^{\flat\prime}$, and $b^{\natural\prime}$, $g^{\natural\prime\prime}$ and $g^{\sharp\prime\prime}$, which produces that thick, jarring effect (especially if the 3rd itself is doubled in the right hand, confirming it as a second 'fundamental'). This is particularly aggravated when these overtones occur in the middle register, where they are more audible. Listening carefully, compare the effect of placing triads in close position in the two registers:

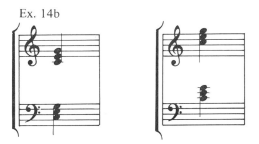

Ex. 14b

This does not necessarily mean that any arrangement is artistically 'right' or 'wrong', though the acoustic effect is factual; but you need to know what you are doing, what kind of effect you *want* to produce and the importance of registers and spacing in achieving various effects. Certainly, if you want to produce clear, clean, lively sounds, keep the spacing as close as possible to that of the harmonic series.

3 Green and White (Grün und Weiss)

German

(i) Discover the pace of change between Tonic and Dominant in this piece.

(ii) On a second playing, see what improvements can be made by intelligent use of registration. This is particularly important where a need for change is felt for rhythmic reasons, though harmonically no change is indicated within your present vocabulary of chords. Always remember in such cases that a certain sense of change can be obtained by change of register. What register is best in bar 1? What register is best in bar 9? Why is this so? (Refer again to the Appendix, page 235.)

43

4 One Man Went to Mow

English Counting Song

One man went to mow, Went to mow a mea - dow, ——

One man and his dog Went to mow a mea - dow. ——

You will need a bass 5th at the beginning of each bar to establish the 'metre' (bar time). Only play two 5ths in a bar if the harmony changes within the bar. Where will you play them then? Play the song and sing the words.

One of the most important things to learn is the *essential integration of harmony and rhythm*—the extent to which harmony is both subservient to rhythm and at the same time helps to define and reinforce it. Sparse harmonies are both harmonic landmarks and rhythmic landmarks. Put a harmony in the wrong place and you may confuse or alter the rhythm. The second bar of this song is a case in point. Learn to discriminate between a wrong note and a right discord. For the latter adds accent, reinforcing emphasis:

Ex. 15a

Not

but

The delayed melodic *a'* belongs to Dominant harmony, but the *b'* has overstayed its time harmonically from the previous beat, becoming an 'accented passing note' (or *appoggiatura*) over the Dominant harmony, subsequently 'resolving' onto the *a'* which belongs to the chord. Such overstaying, especially when the prolonged note is tied, is called a 'suspension'. Not only does one of these versions distort the natural emphasis of the word 'meadow', but it also distorts the musical rhythm, in effect turning the bar into $\frac{5}{8}$ plus $\frac{3}{8}$. For music is as it *sounds* rather than as it looks.

Further Songs

Using Tonic and Dominant 5ths Only

In every case, treat as follows:

(i)   Play the melody.

(ii)   Establish the chord changes, only repeating any chord when metrically necessary—usually the first beat of each bar.

(iii)   Replay the song, adding any desirable improvements of registration and rhythm.

Never *write* the chords under melodies, by any sort of sign (though it is sometimes wise to pencil in phrase marks), because:

(a)   You would rely on what you had written, instead of on listening and thinking, and so lose valuable opportunity for practice each time you play them, and

(b)   When you come to treat the same songs by different sketch processes old marks will either be a nuisance, or prevent your re-listening and re-thinking, either to confirm or improve upon earlier decisions. But you *can* write beside the title of any new melody you discover to be suited to harmonisation with Tonic and Dominant only, 'I/V'; for musicians use Roman numerals to designate a chord according to its place in the scale.

Skip to my Lou
If you cannot remember the tune, refer to page 30.

(i)   Play a bass 5th only when the harmony changes.

(ii)   Incorporate the rhythmic pattern given in the Appendix (page 234).

Spring Song
If you cannot remember the tune, refer to page 32.

Come Home Now
If you cannot remember the tune, refer to page 16.

Captain Morgan's March
If you cannot remember the tune, refer to page 22.

8ve doubling may still be found most suitable for the first phrase.

Anna Marie

Dutch

Oh, where are you go - ing, my An - na Mar - ie? Oh Go - ing to Lon-don the

sold - iers to see, *Hop sa sa, fa la la, An - na Mar - ie.*

Reproduced by kind permission of Oxford University Press.

The Mallow Fling

18th century Scottish

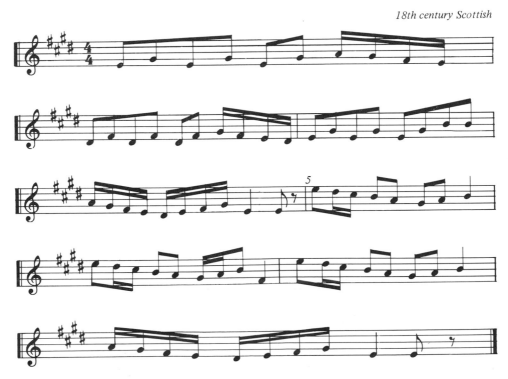

46

I Saw Three Ships

English

The Birds

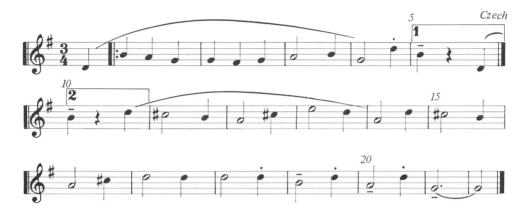

Czech

January Carol

Piae Cantiones 1582

The Farmyard

English

In the first songs used in this chapter harmonies were spelled out in full by the melodic line. You may hardly have noticed that you are by now finding them almost equally easily detectable when only two, and sometimes only one note may be present to suggest each chord. For the melody line continues to imply harmonic relationships. When you make a mistake, your ear tells you that your choice is *not* what you wanted to hear. Have you noticed when this tends to occur? It is on one particular degree of the scale.

Look at bars 3 and 12: each bar could be covered by a single chord, which would include the notes on every beat of the bar. But in one, or perhaps both, cases you may feel convinced that two different chords are needed. The reason is, of course, that the fifth degree of any scale belongs both to the Tonic *and* to the Dominant chord. It is a common mistake of those who work *visually* rather than *aurally* to assume that the fifth degree of the scale requires to be harmonised by the Dominant chord. Sometimes it does: sometimes it doesn't. Make your own decision in these two bars.

Oranges and Lemons

(i)   In the key of F sing, then play, the melody of:

> 'Oranges and Lemons,'
> Say the bells of Saint Clemen's:
> 'You owe me five farthings,'
> Say the bells of Saint Martin's.

Landscape it in 5ths. What happens in the second verse?

'When will you pay me?'
Say the bells of Old Bailey:
'When I grow rich,'
Say the bells of Shoreditch.

What 5ths have you chosen under the word 'bells' here?

Ex. 16a

Bells   of   Old   Bai - ley.

Listen carefully to that sound at 'bells' and decide whether you hear this as a major or minor sound. When you have made that decision, include any other note necessary to define the chord more fully. With which hand will you play it? Why?

(ii) Your reaction if you have played:

Ex. 16b

according to the key signature and failed to raise the lower right hand note a semitone, may further convince you that it is better to omit 3rds of chords than to play a wrong one: for that may lead to your dismissing the entire chord as wrong, and a consequent loss of tonal whereabouts.

But there is no necessity to include more notes than melody plus bass 5ths in the present arrangement. By this experiment you will have understood what you had been hearing, in terms of implied *unstated* notes as well as the essential stated ones.

(iii) In 'Girls and boys come out to play', the first exercise in this chapter, there was no need to decide whether the second verse was *in* the Dominant key, or *on* the Dominant chord, as only the latter was used. But in 'Oranges and Lemons' a move into the Dominant key is firmly established, by use of the chordal relationship I-V-I within each key.

Not only is the Dominant *chord* the next most important chord after the Tonic chord, but Dominant *key* is of equally great importance in relation to the Tonic key. Simple though this inter-relationship may seem in terms of a nursery rhyme, it is nevertheless the very linchpin on which the great structures of classical music depend.

(iv)   You may or may not have noticed how frequently in these many songs you have chosen the chord of V to accompany the 4th degree of a scale. Labelling should follow experience of a thing, not precede it. Play again the first verse of 'Oranges and Lemons' in the key of F. On the 3rd bar you will have:

Ex. 16c

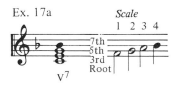

Compare this with the diagram of the harmonic series (page vi), where the *c-g* 5th in the bass implies the close position triad on *c'* above. Above the triad the next note up the series is *b♭''*. These four sounds in the third octave of the series comprise, in close position, the notes of the chord which has especial powers to define a key, the chord of the 'Dominant seventh' (V^7). It is important to remember that *the 7th of the chord is the 4th degree of the scale* of the key:

Ex. 17a

Following the labelling 'shorthand' already explained, a *chord's* number is written with a Roman numeral (e.g. 'V'): additions above a basic triad are written with an Arabic numeral (e.g. 'V^7').

The whole series is now very easy to remember, the *four octaves* consisting of:

Ex. 17b

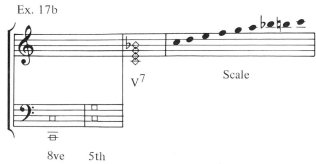

50

This reveals that the harmonic series lies behind dominant rather than tonic harmony.

To help you remember the shorthand for note-names: notes in the lowest octave have capital letters (*C-B*); in the second octave small letters (*c-b*); in the third octave small letters with one upper indicator (*c'-b'*); and in the fourth octave, small letters with two upper indicators (*c''-b''*). (See page vi.)

Owing to its situation in the harmonic series, the power of the Dominant seventh chord is so strong that when root, 5th and 7th are present (as in example 16c) the 3rd will be implied acoustically without being played. You will often notice this, particularly in three-part compositions. A simple way of demonstrating the power of the Dominant 7th chord to define a key, is as follows:

Ex. 17c

Any sharp key would contain what sharp? Any flat key would contain what flat? Therefore this chord can only occur *in one particular key*, the key of C.

Prove the same point in the case of the Dominant 7th chord in the key of G and in the key of F:

Any key with more than one...would contain...? Any key with less than one...would contain...? Therefore...

(v)　In view of the special place of the Dominant 7th in the acoustic system, and its extreme importance in music, from the simplest folk song to extended symphony, it seems strangely irrational that until recently beginners in harmony have not been allowed to use V^7 and have become accustomed to think first, or *only* of the chord of IV to harmonise the 4th degree of the scale. This practice still survives and has undoubtedly caused discouragement to many trying to play by ear. For so many familiar tunes sound quite wrong with the chord of IV where musical memory expects the sound of V^7. It is not surprising that many give up trying to extemporise on the piano or turn in preference to the guitar, where they will be encouraged to commence, as here, with I and V^7.

But, incidentally, it is always better for pianists to talk of 'V^7', a term applicable to *any* key, than to use a letter name, such as 'B^7' as guitarists do. A chord of the seventh on B could be any of the following:

Ex. 17d

Which of these is the sound of V^7?

Cockles and Mussels

If you cannot remember the tune, refer to page 34.

This is the only song that calls for the complicated kind of rhythm suggested in Chapter 2. Proceed from one sketch to another ... for you are likely to achieve better results in the long run if you concentrate on one thing at a time. Notice the melodic appoggiatura on the word 'Molly' in bar 7.

Ex. 15b

Andulko (See the Appendix page 236, for a note to teachers.)

Czech

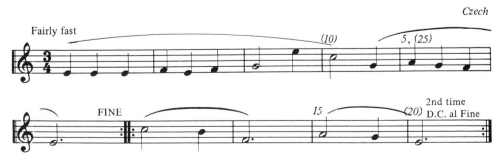

Child beginners should now go on to Chapter 4. Adults may combine the work done on this chapter with the first accompaniment textures in Chapter 9 (which are landscaped on chords I and V only) before returning to Chapter 4.

4 HARMONIC LANDSCAPING: II

Here are two songs you will probably know well enough to play the melodies by ear. If not, they can be found in almost any English school songbook.

1 Lavender's Blue

(i)   Play the melody in the key of F:

> Lavender's blue, diddle, diddle,
> Lavender's green;
> When I am king, diddle, diddle,
> You shall be queen!

(ii)   Accompany the melody with one left hand 5th at the beginning of each line of the song, unless you find more than one to be essential.

(iii)   After you have completed the piece, answer these questions:

    (a)   Can this song be accompanied on a repertoire of Tonic and Dominant chords?

    (b)   If a new chord (a new left hand 5th) is needed, what is its bass note or 'root'?

    (c)   What degree of the scale is that note?

    (d)   Combined with melody of the phrase needing that chord, is the sound major or minor?

    (e)   What chords did you use in the last line of the song, 'You shall be queen!'?

    (f)   Do you find any alternative arrangement acceptable in that last phrase, on the repertoire of those same three chords?

2 This Old Man

(i)   Play the melody, also in F. On what degree of the scale does it commence?

> This old man,
> He played one,
> He played nick-nack on my drum.
> Nick-nack, paddy-whack, give a dog a bone,
> This old man came rolling home!

(ii)   Accompany it with suitable bass 5ths.

The only question in this song is likely to be the harmonic pace at the end: 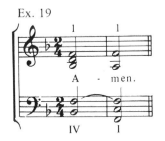. It would be inconsistent to use a quaver pace of harmonic change for the last three notes, when the rest of the piece is landscaped at one chord per bar. Therefore the penultimate chord must come on the penultimate bar. Play the melody notes of that bar and hear how they spell out the chord. But if you particularly want a quaver pace in the last bar, use the 'HXB' bass. Both versions constitute what is known as a 'Perfect Cadence', a phrase ending based on chords V-I.

In both songs you doubtless discovered the necessity to use a bass 5th from *B♭* to *f*, the chord with its root on the 4th degree of the scale, known as the Subdominant (that is, 'below the Dominant') and described with Roman numerals as chord IV.

To use only two or three chords to harmonise a song may seem simple, almost too simple. But even when using only Tonic and Dominant it was found that the melodic 5th degree of the scale could be harmonised by either chord. In such situations only the ear can decide which is right. That is why it is *so* important to play a melody solo first, so that it can convey its own suggestions first, before you start imposing chords on it.

Now that the Subdominant chord is added to the repertoire, a choice must be made in the case of two more melodic degrees of the scale. Occasionally the keynote is open to option: for it is the root of the Tonic chord and also 5th of the Subdominant chord:

Ex. 19

More important is the option for harmonisation of the 4th degree of the scale. For although the 4th degree is the root of the Subdominant chord, it is *also the 7th degree of the chord of the Dominant 7th*. In the key of F:

Ex. 20a

For this reason it is quite a good plan to attempt a first harmonic sketch on a repertoire of I and V only. You will soon hear if it becomes inappropriate.

Train yourself not to jump to the conclusion that a 4th degree automatically calls for the chord of IV. In 'This Old Man' bar 4:  you will have used V. But when those notes appeared in reverse order at the end of 'Lavender's Blue' at "You shall be queen!", which did you choose?

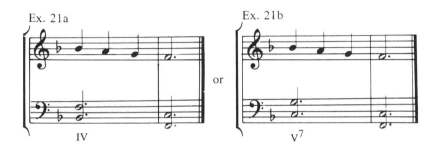

If you tried both, no doubt you dismissed the first. There is however a possible alternative. This allows the bar to commence with chord IV, so long as a change is made on the last beat of that bar to chord V.

Play that version. It is not necessarily superior. The single chord V^7 for the whole bar may be better.

(iii)   Now look again at 'Green and White' on page 43 and find where such choice would have been open to you, had you not been restricted to chords I and V^7. Decide your preference. Either could be defended: one for uniformity with the rest of the piece, the other for contrast at that point in the form of the piece.

The vital necessity, if you hope to gain pleasure and any real usefulness from harmony, is to learn how to choose chords for yourself. Details of how to arrange them is of secondary importance. This is why uniform treatment by 5ths, in addition to its acoustic justifications, is a helpful preliminary. Three stages of experience-cum-study are involved:

(a)   The frequent hearing of actual sounds of chords. Hence the uselessness of instructing beginners to write exercises away from the piano.

(b)   Memory, to recall what sound a known context requires.

(c)   Ultimate development of inner hearing, in terms of the ability to imagine (that is, to *pre*-hear) a harmonic character of sound, detached from context.

3 Ho-La-Hi

Austrian

Now that you have been introduced to the chord of IV through two familiar songs, see if you can hear where it is applicable in what may be new to you, so that you have to use notated melodies. This is not necessarily easier, because written bar lines may tend to handicap recognition of what area of melody belongs to a single harmony.

(i)   Play the melody of this Alpine yodelling song.

(ii)   As a preliminary to harmonic landscaping, play the vocabulary of left hand 5ths you may need in this key. Play them in their order of importance, I-V-IV, returning home with V-I. This corresponds to a designer establishing his colour scheme, and it is a good thing for a beginner always to do this, especially in a new key.

(iii)   Play the melody, landscaped with the appropriate bass 5ths. Notice the importance of correlating structure and pace.

Students using Part II alongside this part can embark on Chapter 10 at this point, or at the end of this chapter.

4 The Smuggler's Song

Cornish

Treat this song by the same stages, (i), (ii) and (iii) above.

(iv)   Play it once with a 5th at the beginning of each bar (more when necessary). Then play a 5th only when the harmony changes. Notice the 'harmonic rhythm' and its contribution to formal structure.

5 The Lincolnshire Poacher

Accompany the first line of this song with landscaping 5ths.

(i)   Make a quick first sketch, without delaying to think theoretically.

(ii)   Assess that sketch. If you are critical, improve upon it.

(iii)   Make a further sketch, with two bass 5ths to each bar.

Here are three different settings. Compare them with your own. Comment on anything that sounds to you objectionable. Can you explain why?

Which of the upper two versions do you prefer?

In bar 2 of the top setting the player has presumed the chord of V for the 5th degree of the scale, having leapt to the conclusion from the first note in the bar, instead of considering the harmonic implications of the bar as a whole. Many listeners will be disturbed by bar 3 of the same setting. Why?

It should not be assumed that licence to use a continuous strand of 5ths in the bass such as I have advocated means that 'anything goes' in the way of such parallel shifts in the web of sound, the bugbear of harmony students down the ages known as 'consecutive fifths' and 'consecutive octaves'. On the contrary, the transparent texture provided by this sketching process shows up errors of parallelism so that the student learns to *hear* them, instead of 'combing through for 5ths' for no better reason than that they are 'against the rules'. That is too often done without any understanding of which parallels are displeasing, and why.

In so far as 5ths have been used consistently as a *unit*, as one strand of a textural web (like a doubled pair of threads forming a thick border at the base of a piece of weaving) they have generally been acceptable: that is, so long as that bass provides a counterpart to the melody, the two dovetailing to form an agreeable, if simple, texture.

In bar 3 it is not the bass 5ths in themselves which displease, constituting the fault known as consecutive 5ths, but parallel 5ths (and 8ves) between bass and melody which disrupts the texture and weakens it. The fault stands out objectionably to the ear as the visual equivalent of an error in a darn or in brickwork where, in a pattern which normally alternates between one row and the next, a slip suddenly involves two rows in running parallel, in *haphazard* fashion.

This is most liable to occur between two chords with roots next door to one another, called 'adjacent chords', and when melody and bass move in the *same* direction. As chord IV often precedes chord V, especially at a phrase ending, aural sensitivity to this pitfall is vital, a prior necessity to knowing how to handle the situation.

Bars 3–4 of 'The Lincolnshire Poacher' must therefore be chords I-V-I (or the 'HXB' bass, which has similar implications).

Though chord IV proved unsuitable in bar 3, it could be used as an additional chord in the middle of bar 1, as in the third setting above. From there it moves happily to chord V (in contrary motion to the melody this time) which now becomes acceptable in that bar because the harmonic pace has quickened to two chords per bar throughout.

Avoiding Parallels

In terms of the Present Process

6 In dulci jubilo

14th century German

This tune is still written in terms of the rhythmic notation of its period. (See Chapter 2, page 27.) Landscaping should reveal to the player that, by today's conventions, this lilting melody would be written in $\frac{6}{8}$. Where do you find a need for the chord of IV? If it presents any problems, don't stop, but make a mental note of the phrase involved and continue to the end of the piece.

In 'The Lincolnshire Poacher' parallelism between chords resulted from a wrong choice of chords. But in some contexts IV-V *may* be the basic sound you want to hear. To change a chord merely to avoid consecutive 5ths would be an evasion of musical priorities. A comparison of several vocal settings of this carol shows that some arrangers have had trouble with bar 13.

There are various ways of solving this problem. The simplest solution when both chords are maintained in root position (which bass 5ths prescribe) is to avoid similar motion by dropping the register of the second chord, V. This is a progression frequently encountered in keyboard music; not merely to avoid parallels, but because of its strength as a IV-V equivalent of the 'HXB' bass. It would not be possible in choral writing (on which so much paper harmony teaching is based), because it would involve dropping below the register of the bass voice. It is essentially an instrumental idiom, for piano, bass string or wind instruments.

Landscaping with 5ths should clearly reveal the spots where, if those *are* the chords you want, some skilled manipulation will be needed when it comes to a detailed arrangement. (See the Appendix, page 237.)

7 Sacramento

North American

A - round Cape Horn we're bound to go, *Sac - ra - men - to,* *Sac - ra - men - to,* A -

round Cape Horn thro' sleet and snow *To the banks o' Sac - ra - men - to.*

Blow, boys, — blow, for Cal - i - for - nia, O! There's

plen - ty o' gold, so *I've been told, On the banks o' Sac - ra - men - to.*

This song emphasises the point made in Chapter 2 that *where* is of prior consideration to *what* in the matter of chords.

(i)   Using Tonic 5ths only, where will you play them?

(ii)   What do you learn from this sketch?

(iii) Landscape the harmonies with Primary 5ths, played at minimum necessary places.

This is the most challenging song so far. Some people who have done quite advanced written harmony find it difficult. Yet some beginners sense quickly *where* should go *what*. Investigate alternative possibilities and give yourself time to do justice to it before comparing your results with the Appendix (page 238).

Important as it is to learn the melodic scale-to-chord relationships, which will then reveal more choices than you might presuppose, you will realise from this song how there are even more possible options as to what chords may coincide with what melody notes. So, even with only three chords to use, in root position, it will be apparent that considerable aural experience, imagination and judgement may be needed to choose harmonies which truly animate a melody. The brain can select the options, but the ear must choose between them.

The Association between Melody Notes and Primary Chords

The fewer the available choices, the less likely you are to make mistakes. Conversely, the more the options, the greater the chance of error. Examine the available choices in the present vocabulary of chords, by relating melody notes to chords, in a diagram. Make this for yourself, so that you understand the logic behind it:

(a)   On a stave with treble clef, write the seven notes of C major scale in ascending order.

(b)   Above each note, number each degree of the scale, in Arabic numerals.

(c)   Use another treble stave below, and write in diamond shapes underneath each Primary melody note—the 1st, 5th and 4th notes of the above scale—the Primary triad rooted on that note, in close position. In the case of the Dominant, add the 7th to complete the 4-note chord.

(d)   Write the applicable Roman numeral beneath each of these chords.

(e)   Relate the two as follows: underneath each melody note of the scale write the Roman number of the chord or chords which contain that particular degree of the scale. Where two

63

Primary chords are applicable, write the more important one first, and the next below it.

(f) The triads in close position are to be regarded as a 'pocket dictionary' of notes in each chord. But for practical purposes of accompaniment they are better thought of in the acoustic order in which they occur in the lower range of the harmonic series. So write them in this open position on a double stave below, using the shapes which denote 5ths or 3rds.

Here is the opening of the diagram, *to be completed in the order of the letter stages (a) to (f) above:*

(b) Degrees of melodic scale:

(a) Notes of melodic scale:

(e) Chords containing each degree of scale:

(c) Three Primary chords in close position:

(d) The Primary chords numbered:

(f) The Primary chords in the lower, open position:

If all notation is then covered over and so excluded from the diagram, leaving only lines (b), (e) and (d), the numerical relationships are applicable to *any* key. The complete diagram will be found in the Appendix, page 239.

Primary Chords

The common description of these as the three primary triads, I, IV and V is based on an arithmetical order, not the logical ordering of music. From every point of view, V is of prior importance to IV, both as a chord and as a key relationship. Think of them in the order I-V-IV.

As we have seen, many traditional *and* composed melodies require harmonisation by chords I and V only, V involving the Dominant 7th whenever the 4th degree of the scale is a principal melody note. There is

64

no equivalent repertoire of music requiring only I and IV. **In a major key all three primary chords are major.** They are the *only* major chords natural to the key, and the few remaining chords are called 'secondary chords'.

It is a subconscious error on the part of many students to confuse the word 'primary' with 'preliminary' and to regard the use of Primary chords as something to be outgrown! There could be no better recipe for musical disaster: for 'primary' in this connection means *of prime importance*. If primary chords do not predominate, the tonality of the piece has been mistaken, or mishandled.

The process of harmonic landscaping by 5ths has the power to act like an X-ray on music and reveal the skeleton behind the flesh of musical enrichment. Not only in very simple pieces, but in more extended movements, it reveals that the skeleton of 'diatonic' (major and minor) music consists principally of the primary chords of the key or keys concerned. However advanced a harmonist or performer, landscaping helps you to see the wood for the trees. The following reveals the rhythmic as well as the harmonic shapeliness of the phrase, showing how the two interact:

Ex. 24   *Melody adapted from Mozart's Piano Sonata K.283*

The diagram on page 64 reveals that *each primary melodic degree participates in two primary chords*. This presents a choice between two chords to harmonise the 1st, 4th and 5th degrees of the scale (a logical situation which further supports inclusion of the full Dominant 7th chord). For this reason, primary *melody* notes should not be too closely associated with the chords of which they are roots. It is this association which so often leads to wrong choices.

While the perceptive musical ear can lead to a successful performance without recourse to theoretical associations, the theory alone is a lame operative without the co-operation of the ear. The intelligent application of both together speeds quick decisions at the keyboard, the theory being called into play at moments of hesitation or error.

Cadences

The word means a 'falling' and is musically associated with phrase endings and, in harmonic terminology, specifically with a couple or so of final chords in a phrase. Unfortunately cadences are often over-emphasised in the teaching of harmony and detached from the general texture of phrases. Cadences may be thought of as punctuation, an integral part of the sense, structure and inflection of music. Just as punctuation marks mean nothing on their own, there is no point in learning cadences in a vacuum. Only in a surrounding context do they have meaning and a particular role to play in musical form. The three principal cadences involve the three primary chords.

There are two 'full stop' cadences:

(a) the **Perfect Cadence**, referred to at the beginning of the chapter in connection with the end of 'This Old Man', in which the final chords are V-I, and

(b) the **Plagal Cadence** consisting of IV-I, which is familiar to many as the sound of 'Amen', quoted on page 56.

There is one 'comma' cadence:

(c) the **Imperfect Cadence**, which is half only of the Perfect Cadence, ending on the Dominant chord V, as in bar 4 of 'This Old Man'.

The Role of the Subdominant

It will be evident from songs studied so far that chord IV is very much subsidiary to chord V. In the songs in Chapter 3 which could be harmonised exclusively by I and V^7 there was sometimes no central contrasted phrase (as in 'Michael Finnigin' or 'One Man Went to Mow'). When there *was* some contrast in a third phrase or section it was very slight, a melodic variant on the same harmonies ('Green and White'), and in some cases the only way of pointing contrast was by registration ('Come Home Now').

In three of the songs introduced in this chapter, it is the Subdominant chord (IV) which provides some harmonic contrast in the latter half of the piece prior to recapitulation (as in 'Ho-La-Hi', 'The Smuggler's Song', and 'Sacramento'). Form, which in Chapter 1 was highlighted by registration, is now beginning to receive some harmonic delineation

In numerous other songs, chord IV is already found in the first phrase, inserted between Tonic and Dominant, often in the shape I-I-IV-V (as in 'This Old Man').

The Advantages of Landscaping in Primary 5ths

1 The acoustic reason for using 5ths has been demonstrated. The landscaping process of using continuous 5ths in the bass at strategic points is musically valid in that it establishes harmonic perspective.

In limiting the choice of available harmonies, landscaping in Primary 5ths simplifies the task by reducing options. Triadic analysis is minimal, as the working upwards of 'root, 3rd, 5th, etc.' is by-passed: the single interval of a 5th defines the chord.

The sparse occurrence of these 5ths allows the necessary time for the player to think of them *as* chords and yet keep the melody on the move horizontally, in terms of the time canvas.

Due to the structure of the harmonic series, a perfect 5th in the bass automatically prescribes a root position. Therefore the player always knows what chord he is using. (For a teacher's note, see the Appendix, page 239.)

2 The use of constant perfect 5ths is equally helpful manually, because the simplicity of using a single interval enables the hand to operate in terms not of two notes but of *one shape*; so fingering problems are avoided. The layout of black and white notes on a keyboard complicates practical harmony. A simple shift of hand pattern will not necessarily produce a similar chord pattern on a different degree. This is one reason why many people find it more encouraging to harmonise on the guitar than the piano. 5ths have an advantage in that the only perfect 5ths in which notes are not *both* white or *both* black, are the pair from B and B♭.

3 In keeping the texture sparse and clear, the process aids the development of aural sensitivity and discrimination.

To sum up, a skill far better under control of ear, mind and hand will be gained if 5ths are conscientiously adhered to, as long as they are recommended here.

Further Songs and Carols

for Landscaping with Primary Fifths

Many melodies may be brought to life by this process with an ease no less surprising than rewarding. Any sketch process may produce a suitable 'performance' arrangement for certain pieces, resources or occasions. For others, an early process *is* simply a sketch for a more detailed version, but it has a vitally important role to play. **BUT** always play the melody solo before adding any left hand part.

John Brown's Body

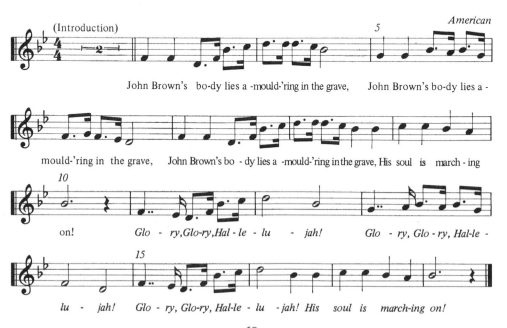

John Brown's bo-dy lies a -mould-'ring in the grave, John Brown's bo-dy lies a -

mould-'ring in the grave, John Brown's bo - dy lies a -mould-'ring in the grave, His soul is march - ing

on! Glo - ry, Glo-ry, Hal - le - lu - jah! Glo - ry, Glo - ry, Hal-le -

lu - jah! Glo - ry, Glo-ry, Hal-le - lu - jah! His soul is march-ing on!

Men of Harlech

Welsh (words by Thomas Oliphant)

Hark I hear the foe ad-vanc-ing, Barb-èd steeds are proud-ly pranc-ing, Hel-mets, in the
Men of Har-lech, lie ye dream-ing? See ye not their fal-chions gleam-ing? While their pen-nants

sun-beams glanc-ing, Glit-ter through the trees.
gai - ly stream-ing Flut-ter in the breeze.

From the rocks re - bound-ing,

Let the war - cry sound-ing   Sum-mon all At Cam-bria's call, The haugh - ty___ foe___ sur -

round - ing.   Men of Har - lech, on to glo-ry! See, your___ ban-ner famed in sto-ry

Waves these burn - ing   words be-fore ye, 'Brit-ain scorns to yield.'

Sweet Nightingale

English

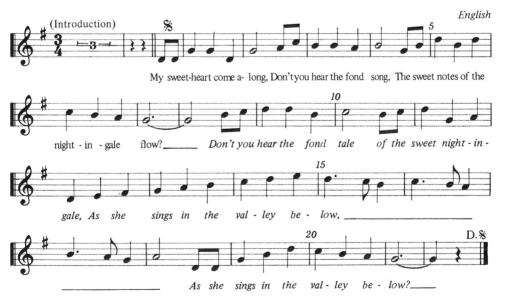

My sweet-heart come a- long, Don't you hear the fond song, The sweet notes of the

night - in - gale flow?_____ Don't you hear the fond tale of the sweet night - in -

gale, As she sings in the val - ley be - low, _____

_____ As she sings in the val - ley be - low?____

69

The Shepherdess

French

(Introduction)

Pulcinello

French

(Introduction)

On Christmas Night (The Sussex Carol)

English

On Christ-mas night all Christ- ians sing, To hear the news — the

an - gels bring, On News of great joy, — news of — great mirth,
bring, —

News of our mer - ci - ful — King's birth.

O Little Town of Bethlehem

English (words by Bishop Phillips Brookes)

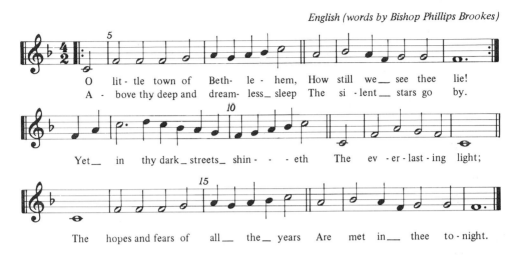

O lit-tle town of Beth-le-hem, How still we __ see thee lie!
A - bove thy deep and dream-less __ sleep The si - lent __ stars go by.

Yet __ in thy dark __ streets __ shin - - - eth The ev-er-last-ing light;

The hopes and fears of all __ the __ years Are met in __ thee to - night.

The Holly and the Ivy

English

The hol - ly and the i - vy, When they are both full grown, Of __

all the trees that are in the wood, The __ hol - ly bears the crown:

O the ris - ing of the sun __ And the run - ning of the deer, The __

play - ing of the mer - ry or - gan, Sweet sing - ing in the choir.

Fire Down Below (see page 21)
The Ash Grove
Angels from the Realms of Glory
Ding, dong! Merrily on High
The Cuckoo
Rio Grande
Bonnie Dundee

Beginners should go on to Chapter 5. Those who are following Part II simultaneously should work through Chapter 10, before returning to Chapter 5.

5 HARMONIC LANDSCAPING: III

1 The Black Nag

(i)   Play this English Country Dance melody. Does anything surprise you?

(ii)   What is the tonality or key?

(iii)   A key signature never defines a key: it only provides clues. This signature of B♭ could indicate F major or D minor. Could it be anything else? How can you find out?

(iv)   Play the scale of the piece. This necessitates finding what sounds to you to be the 'home note' of the melody: then play, in ascending order, such notes as occur in the piece. Write down the scale you find.

(v)   Those who labelled the key 'F major' or 'D minor' were reasoning theoretically from visual evidence. The student who suggests 'G minor' is using his ears: but he will have expected an E♭ in the key signature. As evidence, search the piece for an 'E', 6th degree from G. A scale is not only an instrumental exercise. It is a 'sound scheme', equivalent to a colour scheme which may be daubed in blotches at the side of a picture or printed on the selvedge of furnishing material. There is no obligation to use a shade of every existing colour, nor in any melody a note for every letter-named degree within the octave.

The scale of this melody may therefore be either:

Ex. 25

or

These are the scales of the two most prevalent of the mediaeval 'modes', tonalities with a distinctly different flavour from later 'diatonic' major and minor keys. Notice that both have a tone between the 7th and 8th degrees and that only the 6th degree is different between the two.

Can you discover what note to start from, in each case, to reproduce the identical pattern of tones and semitones of those two scales, *using white notes only*? Observe the interval pattern of the first three notes before you start, as this will shorten the search.

The name of the first white note is also the initial letter of the mode. Which white note started the first of the two patterns? 'D' stands for Dorian mode, in which the distance from the keynote to 6th degree is major. The second pattern started on the white note 'A': in the Aeolian mode the sixth is minor. Modes can be transposed in the same way as any other scales: the pattern of intervals remains the same. Remember that the 6th degree is the only difference between these two modes, and that the names are 'Dorian' and 'Aeolian'.

But in 'The Black Nag' there is no 6th degree, so it is not possible to specify which of those two modes it is in. But the F natural in the second line defines this 'minor-sounding' piece as being in one of those two early modes, as are very many folk songs and dances, a wealth of musical material too long denied to the elementary harmonist under the misconception that modal harmony is only for the advanced musician.

(vi) Establish pace and style with a Tonic 5th. The title of the piece is a clue to both. Only change the 5th when you find it essential to do so: maintain Tonic 5th as long as it is acceptable.

(vii) You may not have noticed consciously before that the leading note (7th degree of the scale) is **the 3rd of the Dominant triad**. So when the 7th degree is a whole tone instead of a half-tone below the keynote as in these modes, it makes the Dominant chord minor, as you will have heard in the second line of 'Black Nag'.

The whole piece can be successfully treated on the chords of I and V in the mode. But in view of the fact that both these chords are minor, one might relish a ray of sunlight in the form of brightening to a major chord somewhere in the second part. Can you suggest what 5th you would use to establish the chord of your choice?

You will recognise that for much of the way complete triads are spelled out by the melody, leaving no sensible place for an option. Your insertion of a major chord will be striking, and will produce a 'harmonic accent'; so don't throw it away in an odd corner, but place it where melody and rhythm justify accentuation. On what degree of the mode's scale are you basing your major chord?

(viii) Play the whole piece through, and then transpose a tone up (very easy), and a tone down.

Alternative Chords of Opposite Character

(i)   In the second section of 'The Black Nag', G minor and D minor triads are completely defined for eye and ear by the melody until the end of the sixth bar. Then follows a weak-beat scalic triplet leading up to a strong-beat scalic triplet. This particular passage held the strongest accent earlier in the piece and now marks the turning point for home. You probably treated the strong-beat triplet as part of G minor. But if you repeat it with no bass beneath it you may hear a different harmony:

It may begin to sound as part of a major chord instead of the previous minor chord.

(ii)   It is important to recognise that the essential interval of a Perfect 5th which bounds the close-position triad of the majority of chords contains within it two intervals of a 3rd: and that these two 3rds are always opposite in character, one major and one minor. To clarify this visually on the page, smaller notes are used for minor thirds in this example:

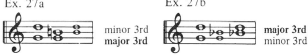

Ex. 27a   minor 3rd   Ex. 27b   major 3rd
major 3rd   minor 3rd

Therefore any passage of melody covering the area of a 3rd is potentially open to interpretation *either* as the upper 3rd of one triad *or* as the lower 3rd of another triad. And these two chords will always be of opposite character:

Ex. 27c   may indicate   Minor   or   Major

This fact is of prime importance in modal music.

(iii)   It is essential to listen to an area of melody *without any bass* to decide in which light you hear it: for once you have successfully presented the passage in one light it may be difficult to 'un-hear' it that way.

(iv)   To clarify examples in notation, small-note 5ths will indicate minor chords as in example 27c. The defining 3rds in each case will, of course, be stated or implied in the *melody*; for, as already emphasised, 3rds do not sound well in the bass between root and 5th. In this particular context, in the penultimate bar of 'The Black Nag', the alternative to the minor chord on the home note of the mode (Chord I) is the major chord on the third degree of the scale (Chord III). It is one of the most important chords in the Dorian and Aeolian modes.

2 What shall we do with the Drunken Sailor?

(i)   Play the melody. Is the key signature correct? What mode is it in?

(ii)   Accompany the song with the 5ths that sound right to you, placed where you think fit. Notice the particular accent to be felt on the word "Early" and see if you can bring this out harmonically. After you have made your choice, examine possible alternative harmonisations for that bar, as there are several.

(iii)   This melody does contain a 6th degree, which defines the tonality as Dorian on its traditional home ground from D-D; so the B flat key signature found in many editions (provided only to be contradicted) is putting old wine into new bottles! A particular flavour of that old wine is apparent in the first two pairs of bars which exemplify modal folk music at its most primitive, with the adjacent and parallel chords of—in this case—D minor and C major. No student will doubt the dictates of his ear that this is what he wants to hear in the context, but some may anticipate a reprimand for using 'consecutives'. What chords of the mode are these two? What chords would they have been, had the key been C major?

This feature of modal music is extremely important to grasp aurally; for style is not a matter of disconnected rights and wrongs but a question of *relevance to context*. Most tonal music consists of the same six or seven chords, rooted one on each step within the octave, and it is the relationships of these chords to each other which differentiate one kind of tonality from another. The important thing about those adjacent D minor and C major chords is that they are chords I and VII in the Dorian Mode (based on 'D') and *not* chords II and I in C major. Used in that way in a major key (a very common error) they would constitute a wrong choice of chords, not relevant to the context, because the tonality would become momentarily modal. Nor, even in the modes, do they very often occur in quite such primitive parallel fashion, here suggesting the drunken lurching of the sailor in a somewhat primitive condition!

(iv)   After the obvious treatment of the first three pairs of bars, bar 7–8 will need more careful thought. The vital thing is to *omit all bass* and *listen to the harmonic implications of the melody*. Play the first two quavers of bar 7. Do they sound major or minor? Remember that this is not a question of whether the interval itself is major or minor (as each kind of triad contains both kinds of 3rd) but a question of whether you hear the melodic line as part of a major or minor harmony. Listen to the second pair of quavers in the same way. Alternatively, treat all four quavers together, as expressing one harmony.

(v)   How many alternative settings can you find for the cadences? Which do you prefer? How many chords have you needed to harmonise the piece, and on what degrees of the mode are they rooted?

(vi)   'The Black Nag' was satisfactorily harmonised on chords I and V of the mode (both chords minor). The 'Drunken Sailor' can be entirely set on the surprising vocabulary of chords I and VII (the latter major). But it is more interesting with a couple of chords in bar 7. The Appendix (page 240) shows various possible settings.

Primary Modal Chords

The 'Drunken Sailor' introduced the four principal chords of Dorian and Aeolian Modes in a familiar context. As none contains the variable 6th degree, all four apply equally to both modes:

Ex. 28

Regard D as the home note of either mode and write the appropriate Roman numeral beneath each of the above chords. Then write the equivalent chords (for either mode) with A as the home note. These four chords are as important in the Dorian and Aeolian Modes as the three primary chords are in diatonic major and minor music. Clearly they are, as a group, notably different from those primary chords and indicate why modal harmony has such a special character, the juxtaposition of major and minor chords resembling an ancient crown in which sombre stones are mixed with bright jewels. Sometimes there are groups of each and sometimes they come one at a time in an unexpected way.

3 The Tailor and the Mouse

There was a tai-lor had a mouse, Hi did-dle un-kum fee-dle! They lived to-ge-ther in one house, Hi did-dle un-kum fee-dle! Hi did-dle un-kum ta-rum tan-tum Through the town of Ram-say, Hi did-dle un-kum o-ver the lea Hi did-dle un-kum fee-dle!

(i)   Which mode is this song in?

(ii)   Set it with 5ths as you think fit, using not more than one per bar. Afterwards, consult the Appendix, page 240, for comparisons.

78

4 Greensleeves

There are many versions of this tune. 'Folk' music is performed by ear and varies according to the whim of the performer, which accounts for melodies surviving in different written versions. Composed 'art' music is written and then performed, which makes for greater degree of uniformity ... though performances must also differ. Notation took time to develop and is still developing; but today we are at least accustomed in tonal music to pitch notation being accurate within a semitone. In the modal period certain semitone variations, ('decorations' of the basic scale) were performed but not necessarily notated. This practice was described by mediaeval theorists as 'musica ficta'.

(i)   Play the melody as it is written above.

(ii)   Which degrees of the scale are subject to such variation, according to the versions of this melody you have heard? To which mode would you attribute the song?

(iii)   Landscape the harmonies with the minimum necessary bass 5ths, using the version of the melody you prefer.

(iv)   By now you will probably have made the following discoveries:

    (a)   that harmonic landscaping in 5ths accommodates any version of the melody, because the variants do not affect the basic skeleton of the piece: they only concern 'passing' notes, mainly upper and lower mordents (alternations between a principal note and the note above or below).

    (b)   that the semitone variations concern the 6th degree, illustrating the general tendency to confusion and vacillation between the two modes, and also the 7th degree.

(c)   that, as the 7th degree constitutes the 3rd of the Dominant chord, the entire character of the Dominant chord is changed by the raising—or not—of the 7th degree. So chord V appears sometimes as a minor chord, sometimes as a major.

(d)   that such flexibility of the 7th degree *within the Dominant chord* in no way affects the stability of the *major chord of VII* (on the lower 7th degree) in a modal piece, nor the *major chord of III* (which includes that lower 7th degree). The very existence of these two powerful major chords in the modes is dependent on the 7th being a whole tone below the keynote.

(v)   It is important to gain insight into this modal flexibility in order to understand how the modal system evolved into that of the diatonic minor and to sense the differences between the two.

In this connection there is one further point to be considered. How do you hear the final chord, in which no 3rd is present?

Ex. 29

Historical practice is interesting here. The harmonic series exhibits a major 3rd as the ringing overtone of any perfect 5th. As the sensitive ears of musicians in the modal period (and considerably beyond) recognised a clash with natural acoustics if a piece ended with a minor 3rd, it was common practice to state no 3rd at the end and simply use a bare 5th, as above. However, if you add a major 3rd, a $g^{\sharp}$ in your right hand under that final e', you will be putting into practice another aspect of 'musica ficta' known to historians as the *Tierce de Picardie*. (Tierce means '3rd': the reference to Picardie has not been satisfactorily explained.) Opinions may differ as to when this is or is not suitable and decisions require careful listening. Decide for yourself whether you like it in the last bar of 'Greensleeves' or not.

A valuable exercise is to play a fifth then sing either a major or a minor 3rd within it listening carefully to the difference:

Ex. 30

Play   Sing   Play   Sing

(vi)   An optional extra challenge is to set 'Greensleeves' with two different 5ths per bar (except at cadences). This entails making use of the 'alternative 3rds' concept. What will be your second chord in bar 3? How does this affect the question of what mode the piece is in?

Note that this does not stop you from using 'musica ficta' on the 6th degree in bar 1.

5 The Oak and the Ash

English, North Country

This very emotional song is one of the easiest to do.

(i)   Play the melody. Modify the 7th in the final bar and decide which inflection of it best contributes to the feeling of nostalgia for home.

(ii)   Landscape the song with one 5th per bar. Do not be careless about the anacrusic structure of the phrasing whereby each 4th beat belongs to the ensuing bar. A 'crusic' rhythm starts on a strong beat, an 'anacrusic' rhythm on a weak beat leading to a strong phrase, which normally ends early to allow another similar shaped phrase. Therefore each 4th beat should have a rest beneath it, and each bass 5th lasts a dotted minim, not a semi-breve. This is especially important at the end of bar 4, where the melody of "She wept and she sighed" should be carefully listened to before a 5th is added.

(iii)   The grouping of the principal modal chords in bars 5 and 6 might still lead you to label the song as diatonic minor rather than modal; however there are alternative choices of harmony for bar 2, one of which will firmly establish it as modal. Can you find the two alternatives? (They are given in the Appendix, page 242.)

It is essential to listen to the melody of bars 5–6 before adding any bass (or 5ths on C and F may lead you into no man's land). In this central section the grouping together of chords III and VII suggests an Imperfect cadence in A♭ major, as the intelligent student will perceive. You may play:

Ex. 31a

III   IV   VII

Consider then whether the harmony produced by the B♭ 5th at the beginning of bar 6 is heard as major or minor. Add the respective 3rds to make the chord 'major' or 'minor' in turn and decide which you prefer. A major chord effects a brief modulation into E♭ major. Some will feel this destroys the modal character. Why is this?

It has been seen that the 'musica ficta' raising of the 7th degree of a modal scale makes the Dominant chord major.

Ex. 31b

V7   I

Nevertheless, the chord of the *Dominant 7th in E♭* (clinched by the melodic $a^{♭\prime}$ here) is a sound quite alien to the modal style. This is a diatonic style of modulation, whereas if $d^♭$ instead of $d^♮$ is played at that point modality is beautifully maintained, with a typical mosaic of alternating major/minor chords in 'root' position. The chameleon chord of E♭ now sounds more like VII in the F mode than V of A♭ major. Relish the nostalgic sob of the flat 7th lower mordent in the final bar.

6 The Animals Went in Two by Two
If you cannot remember the tune, refer to page 18.

This is one of the most important tasks in the chapter. It is easy to find chords that will merely 'fit'. But there is a very neat logic of chord groupings to be found, to which 'The Oak and the Ash' may have provided a clue. This will indicate how the modes began to evolve towards the diatonic system.

(i)   Landscape with minimal 5ths.

(ii)   Texture as a vivacious march by registration of the 5ths, not necessarily on the same pattern throughout. Then look at the Appendix, page 242.

7 Belle Qui Tiens Ma Vie (Pavane)

You should now be competent to tackle this slow and stately court dance, one of the most famous and beautiful pieces in the world:

(i)   Play the melody. (Be careful to play the last phrase accurately.)

(ii)   You will be wise to commence by landscaping the first line in large scale terms, using only one 5th per *4-bar phrase* (sustained, or repeated in the rhythmic motif you used for 'Papa a du Tabac'). What does this reveal?

(iii)   Landscape the whole piece with one 5th per bar or, if you occasionally feel the need, a change at the half bar (i.e. within the bass rhythmic unit). If you find bar 6 difficult, leave it unaccompanied and settle the final cadence, bars 15–16, using one chord per bar; then treat cadence bars 7–8. Can you see any connection between the melody of bar 7 and bar 6? If so, you should now be able to set the problem bar. It is often helpful to skip a problem patch and subsequently work backwards in this way. How would you label the chord in bar 7? How would you label the chord in bar 6? There are some alternative possibilities in both lines. Comparisons between the settings of various members of a group will bring these to light.

(iv)   What mode is the melody in? When you came to *harmonise* the tune, where was this perhaps contradicted? What was the function of the chord concerned, at that point? Nearly all the 7th degrees in the melody are sharpened. When an F natural is used in the harmonisation, what particular function does that note or chord have?

   The answers to these questions will show how, viewed in the light of history, the harmony of this Pavane may be seen as early diatonic harmony.

   The modal *chords* I and III have expanded into diatonic *key* areas of minor and relative major. The segregation and intensification of tonal contrasts makes possible the development of extended forms in the 17th and 18th centuries.

   Yet this 16th-century Pavane is still definitely a modal melody as bar 14 shows conclusively. Its Simple Binary (two-part) form expanded in the later diatonic period into what is variously known as Compound Binary form, Sonata form, or First Movement form. The gradual evolution of this form can be viewed historically as through the wrong end of a telescope. In Chapter 1, the germination of the form was seen in the melodic shapes of pieces such as 'Three Blind Mice' and 'Come Home Now', consisting of statement (sometimes in two sections) with repeat. (First Part.) Then development, and finally short recapitulation of statement without repeat. (Second Part.) Altogether *three* areas in *two* sections, of which the second section may also be repeated. In this Pavane may be seen the emergence of the harmonic system which made possible the enlargement and enrichment of that formal structure *from within*. In the first section, the modal chords of I and III here became phrases in keys I and III, with the possibility of the first phrase 'modulating' into the second key on its last two notes. The second main section starts in the second key and returned to the original key.

   The establishment of III major as a *key* favours the ascendancy of the Aeolian Mode over the Dorian, because the chord rooted on the flatter 6th degree (E♭ in this case) becomes needed as the Subdominant, chord IV of that major key. That same 6th degree is also the 3rd of the Subdominant chord of the tonic minor key. The Subdominant chord has been notably absent from most of the modal pieces previously studied in this chapter (together with a quite common absence of any 6th degree in the melodies). But although the melody of this Pavane is manifestly Dorian (bar 14) you will have found the need for a 5th on E♭

in bar 6 (chord IV of B♭ major). So *both* 6th degrees are essential to this piece.

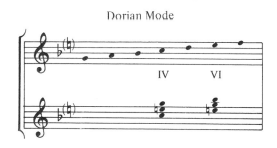

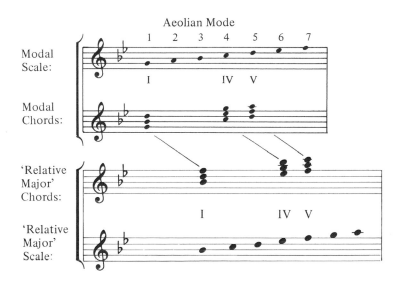

(v)   When you have finalised your version, play it also a tone higher, in the mode on A, then perhaps lower in the mode of F.

(vi)   In the Appendix, page 243 you will find a 16th-century and a 20th-century arrangement of this piece. Which version do you prefer?

8 Dargason

(i)   Here is a strange one! This country dance goes round and round and never seems to come to an end. What do you think is its home note? Despite the prevalence of F major, does the sequence of implied harmonies, melodically expressed, convince you that the piece is no ordinary major tonality?

(ii)   When you have landscaped the harmonies, give the dance a texture suited to its character by registration of the 5th, as in 'Girls and boys come out to play' (page 37). Then compare the effect of a G 5th bass in bars 3–4 with the effect of a C 5th in those bars. What chord does that produce, and what effect does it have on the tonality? Each of these two versions will show you clearly that what is right in the one tonality is wrong in the other. C 5th is, however, acceptable in bar 8 in a modal setting—and it *is* a modal piece—but *not* in bars 3, 4 or 7.

In his *St. Paul's* Suite Holst combines this dance with the melody of 'Greensleeves' going twice as slowly. Hear this if you can.

Further Songs

Rare Turpin

Down in Yon Forest
Searching for Lambs
We Three Kings
Wassail Song
Wraggle Taggle Gypsies

Those following Part II simultaneously should work through Chapter 11 before returning to Chapter 6.

6 HARMONIC LANDSCAPING: IV

Many people find minor melodies more difficult to harmonise than major ones. But the problem is simplified when you appreciate how diatonic minor harmony evolved from the modal system of vocal harmonisation, as you have seen in the previous chapter. Admittedly, minor harmonisation is generally more complicated than major, but it is all a matter of listening and thinking in the right way.

If you combine the Aeolian Mode and the Dorian Mode, and include the 'musica ficta' raised 7th, this is the resulting scale:

Ex. 33a

(Dorian tails up, Aeolian tails down)

or, written another way:

Ex. 33b

(Remember that the Pavane contained *all* these degrees.)

Play this in any rhythm: white and black notes are only used here for visual clarity, the white notes being the constant degrees of this combined scale, which constitutes the 'roll call' of notes for diatonic minor music. Impress on your mind again that **only the 6th and 7th degrees are subject to variation**.

(i)   Play the latter minor scale from C, A, G and E.

(ii)   If you have struggled with various forms of minor scale in instrumental practice—'harmonic minor' and 'melodic minor', the latter in two forms 'ascending' and 'descending'—recognise that they simply involve specific choices between the alternative 6th and 7th degrees. While working on the previous chapter you may have recognised that the descending melodic minor scale *is* the Aeolian Mode: and that it is the Aeolian key signature which is always used for diatonic minor music. Harmonic and melodic minor scales are not much help in handling minor harmony, which is dependent on a much more subtle analysis of melodic context.

(iii)   Choose any minor key. It does not matter which form of the scale you think of. With your left hand, play the Tonic 5th. To what extent does it differ from the Tonic 5th of the major key on the same keynote (known as 'tonic major' key, as opposed to 'relative major')? Make the same comparison between Dominant 5ths of the minor and tonic major key: then between Subdominant 5ths.

Your answer will explain why it did not matter which form of the minor scale you used. For, as when landscaping in major keys, you can leave it to the melody to imply or define the 3rd of each chord: and this will very conveniently take care of just those degrees of the scale which are open to variability. So the basic Primary 5ths will be exactly the same as in the tonic major key.

1 Charlie is my Darling

Before you play the melody, see if you can write it out by memory. Use a key signature of three flats. Think carefully whether the time signature of the Scottish marching song should be simple or compound quadruple. If you are working alone and are sure you cannot remember the tune, you will find it, with a note to teachers, in the Appendix, page 245.

(i)   Play the melody.
Add a left hand accompaniment of minimum necessary Primary 5ths to the *first 6 bars only*. Note any evidence of what has been said above with regard to 6th and 7th degrees and melodic statement of 3rds of chords.

90

So far, it appears that Primary landscaping is just as simple in minor as in major pieces: and up to a point it is. However, it is rarely as simple as that for an entire piece.

(ii)   Continue to landscape this song, from the end of bar 6. Play the melody of bar 7, listening carefully to hear what chords seem to be implied. What kind of cadence does this constitute?

What kind of cadence occurs in bar 8? Sing the 3rd of the final chord without playing it.

From the evidence of bar 7, can you explain why, when modal music developed into diatonic music, the Aeolian Mode triumphed over the Dorian Mode? What would you have named the two chords in bar 7 in modal music? What would you name them here?

With regard to the 6th and 7th degrees of the scale of C minor, as they occur here in bar 7, do you see that *in this context* there is no problem as to whether they should be raised or lowered? It is simply a matter of recognising changes of tonality in the melody.

(iii)   Texture the whole as a lively march by changing register of the 5ths at a crotchet pace, with a crisp touch.

(iv)   Play that bass alone, alternating left and right hands, while you sing the melody. This enables non-pianists to give style to the piece while maintaining pace. (Never let the melody slip into $\frac{12}{8}$.)

In modal pieces the principal chords comprised a mixture of minor and major. But in diatonic keys the principal skeletal chords are birds of a feather. In major keys all primary chords are major. And in diatonic minors, although the dominant chord is almost invariably 'majorised' it is necessary to recognise that this still has to be done by the insertion of an accidental to raise the 3rd of the chord (7th of the scale). For, basically, in minor keys, all three primary chords are minor. It is important to keep this in mind, because the *related keys*, Dominant and Subdominant, are *minor keys*. A little thought about the key signatures of C minor, G minor and F minor—as compared with those of C minor, G major and F major—will confirm this statement. The raised 6th may occasionally appear as a harmony note, but is more likely to be a passing note, as in this song. (Did you remember to write ♮ before *a'* in bar 7?) See the Appendix, page 245 for further details.

2 The Miller of Dee

19th century Scottish

There was a jol - ly mil - ler once Lived on the riv - er
worked and sang from morn till night, No lark more blithe than

Dee,_____ He he._____ And__ this the bur - den

of his song For e - ver used to be, _____ 'I

care for no - bo-dy, no, not I, If no - bo-dy cares for me.'____

(i)   Landscape with 5ths, arranging registration in a shapely way where the vocabulary of chords is repetitive.

(ii)   Name the chords you have used in bars 9 and 10 in terms of modal music. What is their function here?

If you have difficulty in setting bars 11–12, landscape them at first with one 5th per bar, even though you may rightly feel that the harmonic pace quickens here. Two chords in bar 12, I–V, would in any case ruin the verbal phrasing. If you choose only one of those two chords which one will it be?

You will recognise that the melodic $b^{b\prime}$ has now become an appoggiatura, as in the penultimate bar of the Pavane. But where $g^\prime - f^{\sharp\prime}$ was acceptable slurred over the Dominant 5th in the Pavane, $b^{b\prime}$ over that 5th is too bleak a discord to be acceptable here. This can be mellowed by removing the note in the left hand that sounds excessively discordant. For further notes on this song, see the Appendix, page 246.

Summary of the Characteristics of Diatonic Minor Harmony

Studied in correct historical perspective, diatonic minor harmony is seen to derive from an amalgamation of Dorian and Aeolian Modes, with the chords of III and VII firmly segregated into relative major areas, and with the 'musica ficta' raised 7th adopted as the standard 3rd of the Dominant chord.

Diatonic minors, like majors, are based on the skeleton of the three primary chords of I, V and IV, with the Dominant 7th again in the vocabulary (see the last quaver in bar 2 of 'The Miller of Dee'). When played as 5ths in the bass these will be exactly the same as the 5ths of the major primary chords: for all three must still be perfect 5ths, and it is the 3rds of chords which determine whether they are major or minor: and as in major harmonic landscaping that definition is left to the melody. Both the variable degrees of the minor scale are involved only as 3rds of the minor primaries. The 6th degree is the 3rd of the subdominant chord, and the 7th degree—which *in that context* is now almost invariably raised—is the 3rd of the dominant chord.

But this is only half the picture—one aspect of it. For though there are an infinite number of major melodies which do not modulate (that is, they contain no essential modulations) there are very few minor ones which do not, just because of this evolutionary link with the modes. So it may be seen that diatonic minor tonality really involves a double key, a key with two faces. These two faces are not 'harmonic minor' and 'melodic minor': they are 'minor' plus 'relative major'.

In harmonisation, as opposed to technical scale practice, the situation is that the 6th and 7th degrees *behave in different ways*, showing themselves in their different lights according to the contextual flow of the melody, with consequent harmonic implications.

So the greater difficulty in minor harmonisation lies in the higher standard of aural perception that is needed to locate passages in the relative major key, especially when the student is working away from an instrument. Practical experience is essential first.

The scale may now usefully be seen as:

Ex. 34

(i)   Play this scale in all keys.

(ii)   Sing this scale, without recourse to the piano other than for the initial keynote. Sing the ascending 6th and 7th degrees either both flattened or both raised. Repeat from several other keynotes.

(iii)   Look again at both 'Charlie is my Darling' and 'The Miller of Dee'. Can you make any useful observations on the passages where there are accidentals in the melody and the passages where there are no accidentals?

Pocket Dictionary of Chords for Minor Landscaping

Make your own diagram as follows. Copy the double scale in small and large notes, this time based on A minor/C major and rearranged as below:

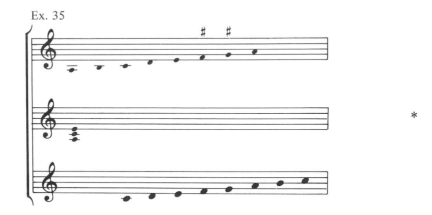

Ex. 35

*

On this stave write the triads on each of the seven degrees (A–G), minor in small notes, major in large, and any other in pencil.

What does the completed diagram clarify?

Modal associations may now be relegated to the past; but those former modal chords of III and VII need to be retained in the mind as part of the basic vocabulary for harmonising minor pieces of music, where they now assume the specific role of Tonic and Dominant of the relative major key. Without needing to attach any Roman numerals to this simple diagram you will be able to see clearly that those six chords (out of the maximum possible seven) consist of the three primaries of the minor key and the three primaries of the relative major.

However, as virtually any melody note may stand *either* as a degree of one scale or of the other in this changeable tonality, no amount of theoretical knowledge will enable you to harmonise a minor piece of music if you cannot recognise the tonal implications of each phrase.

The student whose concept of keys is based almost exclusively on scales and key signatures tends to assume that any change of key will be indicated by accidentals in the melody or require them in the harmony. But the questions as to the placing of accidentals in 'Charlie is my Darling' and 'The Miller of Dee' should have drawn the important observation that modulation to the relative major involves *no* accidentals. It is the home key which requires them.

94

The Form of a piece is also important in this connection (a reason why the setting of mere snippets is such inadequate training in harmonisation). For the haphazard spicing of all areas with strong major chords so typical of modal harmony has gone: and in diatonic minor pieces the major key has a structural role to play in providing a distinct area of contrast in a more or less central section of the total piece.

Although it may not be used at present, the remaining odd triad, doubtless pencilled in your diagram because it is neither major nor minor, needs some explanation here. Its distinguishing feature is that it is bounded not by a perfect 5th but by a 'diminished 5th' (the minor 3rds within it are of secondary importance). It must therefore be the superstructure of some chord that is generated by a perfect 5th. In the *major context* it will be seen that this *diminished triad is on the 7th degree*, the leading note, and that it constitutes the upper part of the Dominant 7th chord, in relation to which it may be viewed as a Siamese twin. For, though examined theoretically in a vacuum a diminished triad appears more minor than a minor triad (*both* its inner 3rds being minor) in musical contexts the ear may rightly diagnose it as a major sounding harmony:

Ex. 36

for this first chord retains its character as Dominant 7th despite the lack of any written 'root' (G). To double the lowest note of the diminished triad on VII means that you will double the 3rd of the Dominant chord V: this is the reason for a rule traditionally taught as an arbitrary dictum. Play the triad in close position and add in the bass each of its notes in turn. Decide which sounds best and which worst.

As the relative minor keynote is the 6th degree of any major scale, it stands to reason that the chord on the 7th degree of that major falls *on the 2nd degree of its relative minor*. You will see from your diagram that this diminished triad on *b'* is on the 2nd degree of A minor and the 7th degree of C major.

It will now be apparent that chords on all seven degrees within the octave have been introduced in this part of the Course, specifically in contexts in which various groups of the six self-standing chords operate as *principal* harmonies. For unless the operation of each group as principal harmonies has been experienced and understood, it is only too easy to misuse the same chords occupying a *secondary* role in another tonality, thereby confusing or even destroying that tonality.

95

3 Czech Folk Song

(i) Play the melody and, after careful listening, set it with a 5ths bass. If you meet any problems apply the 5ths more sparsely, one per phrase instead of one per bar.

(ii) Name the cadences in bars 10 and 12. For further details see the note to teachers in the Appendix, page 247.

4 Two 17th-century French dances

Bourrée

Such a piece can be completely deprived of its correct phrasing, style and pace by harmonisation with a chord per crotchet. This metre should be that indicated by the time signature: two beats in a bar. The rhythmic characteristic of a Bourrée is the anacrusic phrasing, from the fourth to the third crotchet, as in 'The Oak and the Ash'. Some bars will need one 5th and some will need two. When landscaping has been completed, alternative treatments of bars 3 to 4 should be considered, as there seem to be two possible cadences here. Can you find both? In the light of the ensuing section which is more suitable? If you use two chords in bar 3, where should the second 5th be placed? The final four quavers may be set with two crotchet 5ths, so linking the phrase harmonically with the first one. For further details, see the note to teachers in the Appendix, page 248.

Gavotte

The metre is again two beats to the bar. The rhythmic characteristic is a half-bar anacrusis, with a rather self-conscious prancing staccato; so leave anacruses unaccompanied until the piece is well under way. But from bar 6 you may reasonably accompany them. How many 5ths will you play in the first complete bar? You may not be fully satisfied with any solution by 5ths to the end of the second phrase. Settle for what sketches the cadence you choose and after completing your setting consult the Appendix, page 248.

5 Two 18th-century Gavottes (J. S. Bach)

Gavotte 1

from the 'English Suite' No. 3, BWV 808

Gavotte 2 (Musette)

from the 'English Suite' No. 3, BWV 808

Virtually all minor-sounding folk melodies are modal. The modal system is only suited to short pieces. The expansion of the modal system into the diatonic minor/major system was necessary for the creation of extended pieces such as these dances, which you will find quite simple to landscape in 5ths. Add **HXB** bass where suitable. A Musette was a small bagpipe, using a 'drone': so you will know how to treat this melody. Make a list of the many musical features you have studied in Part I which are present in these pieces.

PART II

7 PROCEEDING

The sketching process proceeds. But as new techniques are introduced, those previously studied never become outdated. For the aim is artistic aptness, relevance to context. As in any other art, simple tools are as useful as complicated ones: study of the works of the great composers of any age will reveal this. The constant aim here is to develop sensitivity, judgement and skill, in that order: to which end, listening, thought and executive practice, in that order, are essential.

A bird's eye view of the history of Western music shows that the development of harmony has largely followed the line of ascent of the harmonic series in the choice of intervals preferred in each epoch. Inevitably, as you have read, the first interval widely used was the octave, when men and women sang the same tune. In the Middle Ages, monks in their monasteries and canons in great cathedrals chanted a series of simple melodies, which we now call 'plainsong'. On high feast days or great occasions, choirs might add a second part and they chose intervals of 4th and 5ths, called by the theorists—with some resulting confusion—'organum'. Such organum singing was a closely textured musical fabric, moving mostly note-by-note, and in no way implying chords or keys. In following history and using 5ths in this course, however, you are not copying organum, for the placing of 5ths is seldom note-for-note and they do establish a harmonic skeleton and tonality.

In the later Middle Ages, 3rds and 6ths (inversions of each other, as are 4ths and 5ths) came to be used in church music. (They had long been preferred by folksingers.) So a series of open 5ths and 4ths were first thought old-fashioned and then even ugly. Though not tied to the repertory of those historical periods, this course follows the course of history and gradually extends your knowledge according to the ascending order of the harmonic series shown on the 'ladder' in the frontispiece (page vi): so you now move on to the inclusion of 3rds and 6ths.

1 Mattachins

This is a livelier old French dance adapted from *Orchésographie* (see the Appendix, page 244), by Peter Warlock. You will appreciate the difference in pace and touch quality between this and the *Pavane*; yet a similar rhythmic pattern of tabor accompaniment could be used in both dances. *Mattachins* was a sword dance performed in mock armour as a caricature of a battle.

(i)   After you have played through the melody, work at the first eight bars only:

    (a)   Establish the rhythmic basis with Tonic 5ths throughout.
    (b)   Omit the rhythmic pattern and establish the harmonic landscaping in primary 5ths.
    (c)   Restore the rhythmic pattern to these harmonies.
    (d)   Consider how to justify the repetition of the first line by varying the treatment.

In Chapter 1, it was established that the simplest way to vary a repetition was by changing dynamics. As an alternative or to reinforce the dynamics, you used a change of register. Here you can seek to express change of dynamics also by change of texture, changing the actual notes accompanying the melody. To which is the accompaniment of 5ths in the rhythm ♩ ♫ better suited, the first 8 bars or their repeat? Loud or soft?

(ii)   Play the first line again, loudly, accompanying with Primary 5ths as in i(c) above. Then:

  (a)   Repeat the line softly, enhancing the texture by doubling every note of the melody with a left-hand part running parallel a 3rd below throughout.
  (b)   Repeat it again, this time with the left-hand part a 6th below throughout.
  (c)   Which interval do you prefer? Why?

(iii)   When you have chosen your lower interval, play that lower line louder than the melody and sing it, to hear whether it makes a pleasing part for altos to sing, or second violins (or violas) to play. (This is an important thing to do before you think of arranging any music for others to play or sing: parts consisting merely of odd notes needed to fill in chords considered vertically, moment by moment, are usually very dull.)

(iv)   Although for a performance of the sword dance an identical repeat would be more appropriate, this soft *legato* contrast is undoubtedly a musical improvement from the listener's point of view. What dynamic level do you want for the next 8 bars? What manner of treatment already in your vocabulary might well express this jousting? Funnily enough, being the simplest of all treatments, it is the one most often forgotten! Do you prefer to phrase this section in 4-bar or 2-bar lengths? Try both ways.

(v)   Many simple folk melodies reveal, in embryo, the same basic formal patterns that underlie later extensive symphonic movements. The reason lies in simple human psychological reactions. When you hear something new ('Exposition') you need to hear it twice, if you are to be sufficiently familiar with it to follow subsequent discussion of it ('Development'). But when the original is recalled again ('Recapitulation') to hear it twice more would usually produce a sense of anticlimax rather than culmination. Therefore, in many songs and dances and instrumental works large and small, particularly the familiar 'Minuet and Trio' movements of sonatas and symphonies, the Trio (which is simply a contrasted Minuet) is followed by the instruction that the first Minuet should be repeated *senza repetizione* (i.e. without repetition of the sections).

   This dance follows that form, repeating the first eight bars *da Capo* (i.e. from the head, abbreviated to 'D.C.') *al Fine* (i.e. to the end). See if you can make this a real climax by adding together, simultaneously, *both* ways that you treated the passage in the Exposition. To do this you will have to play whichever interval you chose for the first repetition, with the right hand alone. Then add the 5ths in their first rhythm with the left hand. How satisfactory do you find this?

(vi) Play through the whole piece. Repeat it in the key of G.

(vii) Now look at the Appendix, page 249 to make sure you have understood.

(viii) If you are a string player you might arrange the piece for three or four strings, bearing in mind (iii) above.

If you can get hold of a score or piano arrangement of Peter Warlock's *Capriol* Suite you may see how creating extempore harmonisations along these lines can also help you with sight reading. For the chords you have produced have not been built up, nor should they be read, as vertical units but as two strands of concurrent intervals. The texture in Warlock's score is then thickened by less essential notes. If you understand a basic harmonic structure, you will be able to exercise the musical judgement necessary to decide the *order of importance of notes* in a score, i.e. those which must be played and those which may be omitted.

8   ENRICHING THE TEXTURE: I

In the last repetition of *Mattachins* continuous four-part harmony was produced by combining right-hand 6ths with left-hand 5ths. It was never necessary to break the flow of horizontal musical movement to work out vertically 'root, 3rd, 5th and double the root'. Only *two ideas* were required, one for the right hand and one for the left, each involving a single physical pattern. The two intervals were chosen separately: yet they fitted together. For each by itself fulfilled what were felt to be the harmonic implications of the melody.

The illustration of the harmonic series shows how 3rds and 6ths combine with 5ths in this way, 3rds and 6ths being higher overtones which define more fully the harmony implied by the lower 5th:

Ex. 37

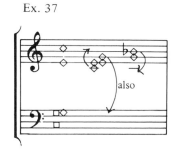

Any triad in close position contains two 3rds, either of which can be inverted as a 6th: and the chord of the Dominant 7th contains *three* 3rds, each of which can be inverted as a 6th. When you harmonise by this means it is, as a general practice, best to start as you have up till now by landscaping 5ths and subsequently filling in right-hand 3rds or 6ths; the latter either running continuously, or occurring sparsely to complete each chord at the moment when a bass 5th occurs. However, this chapter is concerned with experiments in *starting with the upper interval* (3rd or 6th) and fitting 5ths or related single bass notes afterwards. This will strengthen your awareness of the harmonic implications of these upper intervals.

The following examples are largely nursery rhymes, a category of folk song no more to be despised than any other. There are two reasons for choosing them:

(a)   they exemplify certain typical musical 'behaviours' of parts of the scale—stereotypes or clichés which will be better re-membered if learnt in the context of short complete familiar pieces than as isolated exercises, mere potential ingredients. These stereotypes occur in literally thousands of instances in the 'art music' of composers greater and lesser, over at least four centuries. When you have experienced them through simple well-known tunes, you will begin to recognise them aurally in innumerable sonatas, concertos, symphonies, orat-orios, etc. This will further your ability to recognise where to use them when harmonising a melody; and

(b)   at this stage in the course the capacity and confidence to play by ear without any notation, even of a melody, may begin to blossom with encouragement. Therefore in the practical teaching of the work it is advisable to choose simple melodies everyone in your part of the world knows, but in presenting the syllabus in book form here some of the melodies are given for those who may not know them.

Routine for Playing Melodies by Ear

Before proceeding to detailed work on each song, students are advised to prepare as follows.

(i)   When you are going to play a tune by ear, do not start with a shot in the dark at the first melody note. It is most important to establish the habit of first playing the key chord. Always arrange the chord as it would occur in the harmonic series, namely as left-hand 5th plus right-hand 6th with the keynote at the top (a); you will find this far more helpful than (b):

Ex. 38

(a)   not   (b)   or

(ii)   Listen to the chord and *sing* the first note of your tune, mentally assessing which degree of the scale it is, before you play any note.

1 Three Blind Mice and Frère Jacques

In Chapter 1 'Three Blind Mice' was effectively doubled at the octave. Now a couple of richer arrangements can easily be made:

(i)   After you have played the melody through in D, double every note by a 3rd or a 6th beneath it, with the right hand. Stick to one interval as long as it is satisfactory. In the fast part either double every quaver or, if that is too difficult, simply play a lower note at the beginning of each beat.

(ii)   See how this works over a Tonic 5th, played and sustained once for each phrase. To mark the end of the piece substitute the 'HXB' bass in the final phrase.

(iii)   It has been emphasised previously that landscaping 5ths are too strong to be appropriate in close proximity, for instance in beat by beat harmonisations. However, in this case it is a worthwhile experiment to change the 5th under the second beat of the melody. Then add your chosen pattern of upper 3rds/6ths. Do the parts still add together satisfactorily?

(iv)   The point about 5ths in close proximity becomes clear, even when the harmonies are correct, because they impede the pace. However, if single bass notes alone are played, as already in the final bar, the music will flow again. In the last phrase add the appropriate single bass note under the *pre*-cadential "*As* three ...". This will imply chord IV.

(v)   The monotony of the bass can then be relieved by registration. This can either be changed together with the right-hand part on the repeat of the phrase, as in Chapter 1, or the right-hand 3rds/6ths setting can remain centrally placed, the left hand 8-5-1 being placed in a suitably connecting register. Climax can be achieved in the three-fold phrase by changing the bass register on each repeat. Do not forget the possibility of placing it *above* the melody.

(vi)   Treat 'Frère Jacques' the same way. You will probably find you can play the final completed version straight off.

Fun with Cadences

(i)   Replay the final phrase of "As three blind mice" in the key of D with the melody doubled in 6ths over single-note 'HXB' bass line.

(ii)   On completing the phrase you will be playing the Tonic chord of

D. Of what key would that chord of D be the Subdominant chord? Starting with that same chord, now thought of as chord IV in the new key, complete the phrase in the new key. Repeat this process through the full cycle of keys, each Tonic becoming the Subdominant of the key with one more sharp (or one less flat)—the Dominant key of each previous key.

Here is the passage in C sharp; after which it will be wise to think in terms of an enharmonic change (change of notation without change of sound) so that the final chord becomes D flat, Subdominant of the key of A flat. Such things are much simpler to play than to read. You will *hear* that the passage continues to drop a 4th each time (not a 3rd as this enharmonic change makes it *appear* when it is written out):

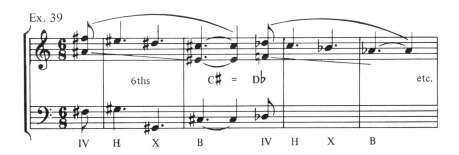

All major scales are made up of two sets of four notes, known as 'tetrachords'. For convenience, musicians refer to the two halves of a scale as the 'upper' and 'lower' tetrachord respectively. In the major scale both tetrachords have the same pattern of tones and semitones:

This does not mean that the upper tetrachord can be harmonised in the same way, as you will hear if you try it!

(iii) Some students may be sufficiently enterprising to try the sequence in minor keys as well. It will not be necessary to think of key signatures: you will only need to get the opening pattern right, then regard each keynote chord as chord IV of the new minor key and copy the sound

108

pattern. For variety, try it with this textural pattern:

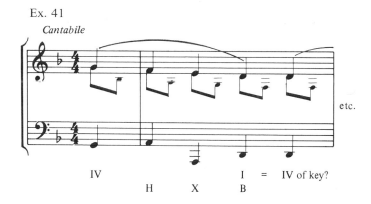

Ex. 41

Cantabile

IV   I   =   IV of key?

               H   X   B

2 Rock-a-bye Baby

(i)   Decide your upper interval for the first two phrases. Play the resulting lower part by itself. What do you notice? Appreciate that such simple logic is more significant than complication. Fit upper intervals to the remainder of the piece. Do not complicate the first half of the penultimate bar, making it awkward to play. The chord is fully spelled out in the melody and only needs one sustained G under that beat.

(ii)   Omit upper intervals and play solo melody over minimum bass 5ths (*i.e.* do not repeat chords unnecessarily).

(iii) Add upper intervals and 5ths together and see if they combine satisfactorily. Use registration intelligently so that bass and treble sound welded, not detached.

(iv) Play the whole in the key of F: then in A flat, or any other keys. The simplicity of the hand patterns will make it easy to remember what you did, and it is technically easy to play.

(v)   Simplify the texture by using the 3rds and 6ths more sparsely. Add them under the melody only at the moments when the 5ths are played in the bass (with one extra 6th before the final note). Play this sparser texture in G: then in the key of F sharp.

(vi)   To make sure you are on the right lines, look at the Appendix, page 249.

3 Marching through Georgia
If you cannot remember the tune, refer to page 31.

(i)   Landscape with Primary 5ths.

(ii)   Not only would it be difficult to double every note in this melody with 3rds or 6ths, but it would clutter and slow it down and therefore be unsuitable. In this and similar situations simply add a right-hand 3rd or 6th beneath the melody note in the right hand at the moment when you play the landscaping 5th.

(iii) In the four chorus bars from "Hurrah!" more is clearly needed. Most important is to add that simple marching treatment of the 5ths suggested in Chapter 2, now with appropriate changes of harmony. Continuous upper intervals also prove both easy and appropriate in this section.

4 Little Jack Horner

(i)   Play the melody: then double it in 3rds or 6ths throughout.

(ii)   Add bass 5ths, ensuring that the two intervals tally and that they produce the sounds you want to hear. For there may be valid alternatives; the choice rests with your own ear and personal preference.

(iii)   Lighten the texture by breaking up each landscaping 5th to form a rocking single note pattern, so:

Ex. 42

(iv)   After you have played your own choice of chords this way, try the first bar treated as IV, then treated as V^7 (upper 3rds over V), then as V^9 (upper 6ths over V). Though the first 6th ($a^{b\prime}$-c') may suggest Subdominant to your analytical brain, it may yet suggest Dominant to your ear. A flat and C are respectively 7th and 9th above the Dominant root, in close position:

Ex. 43

and, although the 7th is here played *above* the 9th of the chord, this accounts for the Dominant sound.

(v)   The rocking pattern must obviously give way to a cadential bass in the last two bars.

Inversions

You may notice that the last five quavers are the same as the 'Rock-a-bye' cadence. Play the first two quavers of bar 7 and listen to the sound they suggest. Is it major or minor? Now play them like this:

Ex. 44

What triad do they now define? They define the triad f'-$a^{b\prime}$-c'': F minor,

111

chord II in the key of this piece. But the bass is not F. Chord positions can change and, in this case, the bass is in fact the *first* note *above* F in the triad. This position is called a '*first* inversion'. Similarly, if C (the *second* note *above* F in the triad) is placed in the bass, the position is called a '*second* inversion':

Ex. 45

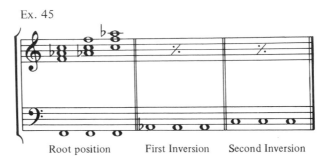

Root position   First Inversion   Second Inversion

The position you have used mainly until now was the 'root' position. To label these new positions, keep the Roman numeral for the chord (in this case, II) and indicate the inversion with the small Roman letter 'b' for a first inversion and 'c' for a second inversion. You have already experienced a second inversion, without calling it anything, in the 'HXB' bass. Example 39 on page 108 could thus be labelled: IV-Ic-V^7-I.

(vi)   In 'Three Blind Mice' and in 'Rock-a-bye', chord IV was only *implied* in the final cadence. To be fully defined this chord needs also the keynote of the scale (the 5th of chord IV) *or* the second note of the scale (the root of chord II), giving the choice of:

Ex. 46

IV   IIb

(vii) Students should be clear that the vital difference between the two chords is that the overall quality of one is major and the other minor, but only *one* of the component notes is different. Therefore, when you are doing aural tests on chords there is no need to seek with the ear four separate sounds. The priority is to hear whether such a pre-cadential chord is major or minor, whereupon the constituent notes will be evident. The difference between an *implied chord* and a *defined chord* is important. The sketch process of 6th plus bass note is very useful because, in the absence of a defining note, it can serve for either of two chords—and may justifiably be heard as either IV or IIb in this case. The governing thought, in either case, is the bass progression of degrees 4–5. Lastly, the horizontal as well as vertical nature of harmony comes to the fore again as we see that a particular harmony may be defined over an area rather than at a given instant. The pair of quaver beats:

both contribute to the definition of IIb, and it would be a musical nonsense to call the second one IV.

Flowing Harmonisation of the Full Descending Scale in All Major Keys

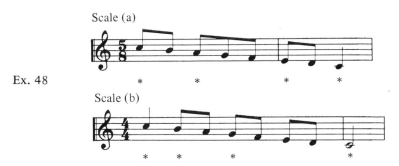

Ex. 48

(i)   Double scale (a) in 6ths. Add single bass notes as indicated by *.

(ii)   Change the rhythm to the more natural pattern of (b) and fit the *same* bass (c-f-g-c) to it, at points marked *. Notice how the accented passing 6th on the second beat propels the downward scale.

(iii) Play this in *all* major keys, progressing in one of the following directions:

    (a)   sharp, moving each time to the Dominant key, *or*
    (b)   flat, moving each time to the Subdominant key.

(iv)   *Students with sufficient keyboard proficiency* may try to progress by rising a semitone with each key change, as would be needed for accompanying the singing of scales. In this case *never* move straight to the

113

key chord a semitone above, which is very ugly and makes it difficult if not impossible for singers to sing in tune. You need to lead into each new tonality and here is a well-tried way. Stabilise the present key by a Plagal Cadence under the sustained note:

Ex. 49

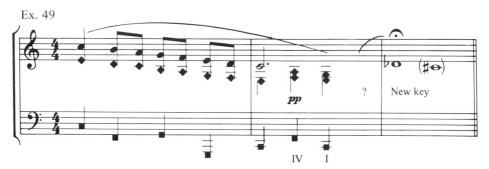

Hold on to that third-beat chord in the second bar while you do some constructive thinking. Which note that you are now playing is contained in the key a semitone above?

(a)   Keep it.
(b)   Drop your left hand *silently* over the Dominant note of the new key.
(c)   Drop both notes of the lower 3rd in your right hand down one semitone.
(d)   Play the full chord.

Your top note has become the leading note of the new key: and you have played a strong Dominant 7th chord to make unmistakable a Perfect Cadence 'modulating' into the new key. Complete it. Then play the scale of that key descending in 6ths, followed by a repeat of the Plagal and modulating Perfect Cadence patterns into the next key a semitone above. Continue through all keys. If you have not fully understood, look at the Appendix, page 249.

5 Early One Morning

19th century English

114

'Oh, don't de - ceive__ me, Oh, ne - ver leave__ me,

How__ could you use_____ a poor__ mai - den so? '

(i)   Landscape in 5ths.

(ii)   Reduce the bass to single notes. Texture the upper part with 3rds and 6ths where you think fit; but do not overload bars where the melody itself spells out a chord fully.

(iii)   What use can you make of parts of the scale exercise you practised in Example 48?

6 Will Ye No Come Back Again?

17th century Scottish

Bon - nie Char-lie's now a - wa,   Safe - ly o'er the friend-ly main,
Mony   a heart will break in twa   Should he n'er come   back a - gain.

Will ye   no come back a - gain?   Will   ye no come back__ a - gain?

Bet - ter loved ye   can - na be,   Will   ye no   come   back a - gain?

This is one of the most important and rewarding songs to do. You will find the need to change upper intervals rather more frequently than in previous songs. Treat line 2 by upper intervals first. Where 3rds or 6ths sound equally valid, fit relevant 5ths to each version and make your choice. Avoid monotony of bass by registration. Notice the natural rhythm of "Better" and "can'na". This rhythm, in which the second of a pair of quick notes is dotted, is known as the 'Scotch Snap'.

7 Hickory, Dickory, Dock!

Hick-or-y, Dick-or-y Dock!__ The mouse__ ran up__ the clock.__ The

clock struck 'One', the mouse ran down, Hick-or-y, Dick-or-y Dock.

(i)   Play the melody. Then double every note with either a 3rd or a 6th, keeping to one interval as long as you find it agreeable.

(ii)   Add a bass part in 5ths or single notes as you think fit. You can make this a continuous 'tick-tock' if you wish, or you can use the rhythm  as in 'Three Blind Mice'. Try both.

(iii)   The third phrase ("The clock struck one") may be improved musically and imaginatively by a change of texture:

   (a)   What chord is implied by this 6th?

Ex. 50

   (b)   What note is missing to define that chord as a first inversion? Include that note, placed in between the two notes of the 6th. Play the lowest note with the left hand and complete the phrase in this pattern of continuous first inversions, which makes a very effective bell-like sequence.

(iv)   Play the final phrase with single bass notes on each beat, under continuous 3rds *or* continuous 6ths. Sing the 'middle' part of each. With 6ths in the right hand, you will hear an *A* underneath, giving you chord V (Dominant in root position); with 3rds, an *a* underneath, forms part of the 'HXB' bass, chord I_c (Tonic in second inversion).

116

(v)   If you tried 5ths in the bass for phrase 3, did you find them satisfactory?

Ex. 51

Scale degrees

etc.

It is important to *hear* the sound of these parallels—and to approve them or not—rather than simply to be told to avoid them. When you *do* want to avoid them, you know from Chapter 4 that you can do so by a change of register if the parallels are between IV and V. But treating the parallels V-IV by changing the register and dropping the bass IV an 8ve is no improvement. So, one of the chords inverted might be a solution. If you try this by using *either* V_b *or* IV_b, you will not find it the best solution: but if you invert them both, making a succession of first inversions as in (iiib) above, you will find they sound very well. A series of first inversions is never disagreeable in the way that parallel root positions are usually felt to be.

8 Upon Paul's Steeple

This final song brings the use of 3rds and 6ths to a joyful climax. Except

117

for bars 7 and 8 and the final cadence (to which the clue is landscaping, at a minim pace) no bass is needed; for the upper intervals alone will best convey the impression of bells. So play the under part with your left hand. Will you choose 3rds or 6ths?

After making your own experiments, consider the following: What would happen to the sound of the bells as the children get nearer to Saint Paul's? The challenge is to convey a sense of accumulating sound without losing the element of repetition. If you make use of the suggestion given in 'Hickory, Dickory, Dock' for "The clock struck One! The mouse ran down," you will be able to develop the treatment, by enriching the descending scale of 6ths with middle notes when it occurs the *second* time. Finger the 4ths in the right hand so:

$$\left\{ \begin{array}{c|ccc|ccc} 5 & 4 & 5 & 4 & 3 & 5 & 4 & 3 \\ 2 & 1 & 2 & 1 & 1 & 2 & 1 & 1 \end{array} \right.$$

The scale may then be further enriched on its *third* appearance, by enlargement of this chordal texture by means of registration, as follows:

(i)   Drop the register of the left-hand note (6th below melody) and repeat the scale.

(ii)   Fill in the over-large space between the two hands by doubling the melody notes with your right thumb. Repeat the scale.

(iii)   Double the bass notes an 8ve below. Repeat the scale and continue loud and full to the end of the piece, with a cadential bass at minim pace.

This cadence provides the clue to bars 7–8. Landscape bar 7 and then arrange it in a crotchet bass, which may be done in various ways. Notice the extended phrase here, which alters the barring for the rest of the piece. These extra three notes generate the additional repeat of the scalic theme: and the harmonic implication here, which prevents that further repetition sounding redundant and renders it *essential*, lies in the implication of 3rds:

Ex. 52

This diversion to B minor, chord VI of the key, instead of the home chord of D major, constitutes an 'Interrupted Cadence' (which

Americans call a 'Surprise Cadence' or 'Unexpected Cadence') after which further continuation is necessary to reach a Perfect Cadence. Interrupted Cadences, especially in short pieces such as folk songs, are always related to the formal shape of a piece; for the unexpected can only be appreciated by reference to an expectation. The practice of learning and using cadences as isolated units, outside a complete musical context, leaves students unaware of their formal significance.

Now you will be able to play the whole piece. Store in your aural memory the rich, bright sound of 1st inversions (especially of major chords) which convey a sense of freedom, of uplift and of leading onwards. This contrasts with the character of root positions, which sound fairly firmly 'seated'—and seated at home in the case of the Tonic chord. On the other hand, 2nd inversions tend to convey a sense of anchoring, of putting a brake on activity. This is their value at cadences, so they need to be avoided or used with care midstream. When a moment of climax is needed, a 1st inversion of the Tonic chord often supplies what the ear wants to hear.

It is very important to develop the habit of playing 1st inversions with the top note (be it root or 5th) doubled at the octave below and *not to double the 3rd of the chord.* Unless you develop this physical habit, and learn to recognise the sound of doubled major 3rds, you may think you have made a wrong *choice* of chord when only the *arrangement* causes the jarring sound. Parallel 5ths in the middle of a chord caused by this kind of doubling, are not displeasing when used *consistently* over a passage.

Further Songs

For Treatment by 3rds or 6ths over 5ths

In most cases landscape before trying upper intervals, until you find you are becoming competent to handle both together from the outset. As a general rule stick to 5ths in the bass, but be ready to change to the single note 'HXB' bass in appropriate cadential bars. You will find most of these very easy. In the first two, see if you can combine both intervals straight away.

119

Away in a Manger

Play the melody by ear, in the key of F, and see if you can harmonise it with left-hand 5ths and right-hand 3rds or 6ths, combining them at the first attempt. If so, you are certainly on the way to harmonising by ear.

In Dulci Jubilo
If you cannot remember the tune, refer to page 61.

Alternative choices of upper interval are often equally good, which in one bar may lead you to want a 5th which is not a Primary. You should remember how to avoid parallel IV-V.

O Little Town of Bethlehem (for melody see page 71)

One choice might again lead to a secondary 5th. If you have problems with "ever*lasting* light" decide which melody note of "lasting" belongs to the chord of the bass 5th. Then add its 3rd under the previous note (appoggiatura). Play the upper interval at "light" with the left hand, instead of the 5th.

The Sussex Carol (for melody see page 70)

A single bass note mid-bar 3 will prove best.

While Shepherds Watched

At "seated" place the 5th high. You might try bar 1 on both intervals, noting the effect on choice of 5ths.

January Carol (for melody see page 47)

Accidentals are not always present, as in the last carol, to indicate modulations. But when they are implied by the melody, landscaping and 'HXB' bass should help you to find them.

Green and White (for melody, see page 43)

The Shepherdess (for melody, see page 70)

Leave the first quaver of each phrase solo.

The Riddle

The first two notes must be solo to avoid the awkward lower part that would result from rising from 3rd of the scale to leading note:

Ex. 53a

The second beat may be the best moment to start doubling here. You will have found this jump more acceptable in some other contexts, at a slower pace and when the bass harmony changed under the second degree of the scale, as in 'O Little Town of Bethlehem':

Ex. 53b

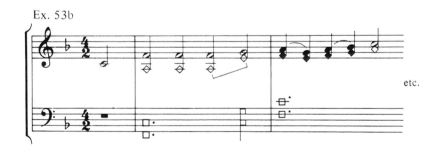

etc.

Men of Harlech (for melody, see page 69)

This song calls for similar treatment to 'Marching through Georgia' (see page 110).

Sweet Nightingale (see page 69)

Don't overload the first short phrase. When there is a long note at "flow" keep the texture flowing by making use of the inner 6th beneath it:

Ex. 54

Donkey Riding

Canadian Sea Shanty

Were you e - ver in Que - bec, Stow - ing tim - ber on the deck,

Where there's a king with a gol - den crown, Rid - ing on a don - key?

Hey! ho! a - way we go, Don - key rid - ing, don - key rid - ing,

Hey!___ ho! a - way we go, Rid - ing on a don - key.

9 MAKING YOUR OWN ACCOMPANIMENTS: I

This chapter is for use in conjunction with Chapter 3, and is concerned with textural enrichment of melodies which may be harmonised by chords I and V only.

1 Joys Seven

You will find you can run through all these sketch processes very quickly:

(i)   Play the *Melody*.

(ii)   Make a *Rhythmic Sketch* by adding a left-hand accompaniment throughout of Tonic 5ths only, placed so as to establish the style and pace of the piece.

(iii)   Following the process of *Harmonic Landscaping*:

    (a)   Establish the harmonic framework, according to Chapter 3, using the 5ths of chords I and V at the minimum necessary places (not more than one 5th per bar). Which chord best emphasises the syncopation under the tied note?

    (b)   Add rhythmic texture of landscaping 5ths by changing the register of the 5ths within each bar, so as to highlight the duple pulse.

    (c)   Provide the simplest possible *independent accompaniment*, while you sing the melody but do not play it: or, preferably, accompany a group of singers, or a player on another instrument. Play only the bass you added in (b), alternating left and right hands. Either hand can commence.

(iv)   Preparing for *Harmonic Enrichment*:

    (a)   First omit all bass. Play the melody and double it at the distance of a 3rd or a 6th below *every* note (as melodies were doubled at the octave in Chapter 1). The only exception should be the anacrusic quaver at the beginning of each phrase, which is best left as a single note. Once you have decided on a suitable interval, stick to it until a change is heard to be necessary. These 3rds or 6ths can be played with the right hand only, or the left hand can play the lower notes (as for two recorders).

    (b)   Play these upper intervals with the right hand and re-introduce the landscaping 5ths. See if they combine satisfactorily or if anything needs to be altered; but use only 3rds or 6ths over 5ths. If this is too difficult for a very elementary pianist to play up to speed, play it slowly. The next arrangement, related to this one, is easier to play.

(v)   Provide an independent accompaniment for a vocal or instrumental solo. Do not play the melody, which should be sung or played by someone else. Base your accompaniment on the rhythm and registration of iii(c). Instead of alternating 5ths, play the bottom bass note only (root of the chord) with the left hand on the first beat of each bar. On the second beat play with the right hand the upper interval (3rd or 6th) you chose above on the word "joy". The 'oom-pah' accompaniment sketched at iii(c) in terms of registration is now more musically expressed.

Keep the setting as simple as possible, only making changes where necessary. Bars 1 and 2 will therefore be the same. On the 2nd beat of bar

3 again use the 6th under "joy". Notice this 6th is next door to the previous one. So make a mental note that a 6th below the keynote may express Tonic harmony: and a 6th below the leading note (7th degree of the scale) may express Dominant harmony. But as 6ths are upper intervals in the harmonic series their effect on their own may be confirmed or contradicted by a lower bass note; hence the importance of landscaping first.

Although in iv(a) you probably changed the interval from 6th to 3rd in the chorus, you will find it satisfactory, indeed preferable, to accompany the entire song with these two 6ths in the right hand, following their respective bass notes.

Recognise the advantage for fluency of not having to think vertically in terms of 'root, 3rd, 5th, etc.'. Only two thoughts are needed for each bar and they are consecutive, not simultaneously required—a bass note followed by relevant 6th.

(vi)   Transpose the independent accompaniment. Your new technique makes it extremely easy to provide an accompaniment for the song in *any* key—much easier, in many cases, than it would be to transpose a melody itself, especially in a full arrangement such as iv(b) above. Play this accompaniment in other keys. See the Appendix, page 249.

Textures for Instrumental and Dance Accompaniments

Carols were originally associated with dancing as well as singing. 'Joys Seven', with its skip rhythm, is typical and the song can easily be textured for a skipping game or dance. Play the Tonic chord of G, with left-hand 5th and right-hand sixth, as at the beginning of bar 1, namely in its position according to the harmonic series:

Ex. 55a

If your hands will stretch the intervals happily, simply break up the chord, arranging the lower three notes to match the rhythm of the melody, note for note:

Ex. 55b

When you reach the Dominant chord, break it up in the same way and complete the carol.

2 Sur le Pont D'Avignon

(i)   Play the melody, then landscape the harmonies in 5ths.

(ii)   Play an independent accompaniment of bass note followed by 6th.

(iii)   To make a new type of accompaniment:

   (a)   Look again at the harmonic series, or preferably play it by memory. By the time it has reached the top of the 'diamond' notes, what chord has been defined? In what key?

   (b)   Play the two *adjacent* notes in the series which, by themselves, can imply the whole chord: ⟨music⟩ then play the nearest pair of notes to imply Tonic harmony (keeping *c″* at the top). If in doubt, play 'Chopsticks'!

   (c)   Play each note separately, starting with the lower, in an undulating quaver rhythm, always pivoting around the 5th degree of the scale. Use this pattern as a left-hand accompaniment beneath the melody, starting with the implied Tonic harmony.

(iv)   To play in duet:

   (a)   While one plays this flowing arrangement, the other player

126

should add the landscaping 5ths underneath, the whole providing a rich texture.

(b)   To make an even richer texture, one can play the 5ths plus the quaver accompaniment, whilst the other doubles the melody at the octave.

(v)   Transpose the whole into the key of G.

(vi)   As with all the other devices recommended in this book, when you have first been introduced to a new one the speed with which you are able to apply it to a new context will depend upon your remembering *what degrees of the scale* are involved. So make a particular note of this now, so that you can apply this two-note accompaniment pattern to other pieces. Then start by applying it to 'Joys Seven' (page 123), adapting it to the key of the piece and to the crotchet-quaver rhythm. This provides a particularly suitable texture for nursery-age children to skip to.

Further Studies in Textures

Apply any of the three textural styles introduced in this chapter to any of the songs in Chapter 3 which were treated with chords I and V only.

The independent accompaniment of bass note and 6th is that most frequently effective. It is no longer necessary—indeed, in many songs it would be quite unsuitable—to double every note with 3/6 before providing such an accompaniment.

So far, in 'Joys Seven', only two 6th intervals have been used: that below the leading note for dominant harmony, and that below the keynote for tonic harmony. You will find that the next two adjacent 6ths can also be used, those under the 2nd and 3rd degrees of the scale in any key:

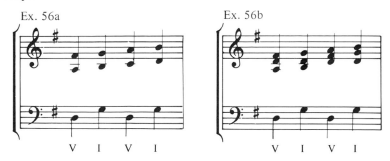

Ex. 56a   Ex. 56b

V   I   V   I   V   I   V   I

Notice how simple it is, for mind and hand, to play (a), compared with (b). There is nothing 'superior' about the thicker arrangement and in many contexts a lighter texture is musically preferable.

3 Michael Finnigin

If you cannot remember the melody, refer to page 38.

Always consider alternative rhythmic arrangements to suit the style and pace, as in Chapter 2. Here try two different paces of 'oom-pah' in proportion to the melody and hear their effect on the speed of the song. You can add more 'zip' by omitting each second bass note, tying it to the first to make the total rhythm syncopated:

The same pattern, with note-values doubled as in (b) makes the pace even faster.

All three treatments of this chapter can be applied to this song.

4 Anna Marie

If you cannot remember the tune, refer to page 46.

Always be sensitive to the importance of rests. Rhythmic vivacity is dependent on 'air' being let into the texture, like a well-risen dough. For instance, in a triple rhythm accompaniment, simple or compound, decide which of these possibilities best suits the context:

Ex. 57c

Which would you choose here for an accompaniment of bass note and 6ths?

5 The Birds

If you cannot remember the tune, refer to page 47.

(i)   Play the melody and landscape the harmonies.

(ii)   Arrange a two-note accompaniment. A rhythmic decision is needed here, as you only have two notes to use and there are three beats in a bar. On which beats are the accompaniment's notes most effective? 1–2, 2–3, or 1–3? Or do you prefer to fill the whole bar by repeating one pair of quavers. You may wish to extend the pattern in the last two bars.

(iii)   Provide an independent accompaniment by playing bass 5ths with the left hand below the two-note pattern played by the right.

6 Andulko

If you cannot remember the tune, refer to page 53.

You may well have chosen to fill the first and third beats in 'Anna Marie', first and second in 'The Birds'. But in this song you may feel that a lively waltz-style filling all three beats is appropriate.

(i)   Play the melody and landscape in 5ths of I and V.

(ii)   Play the first melody note over its left-hand 5th, then take the upper note of the bass 5th into the right hand.

(iii)   Play the single remaining left-hand note, followed by the right-hand 6th once or twice in the bar as you feel appropriate for the pace.

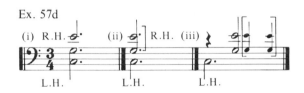

(iv)   Make the right-hand chord fuller by including middle *c'*, which lies under the 3rd finger. Use this chord for all tonic harmony. For dominant bars:

   (a)   drop the left hand to the Dominant bass note.
   (b)   for the two right-hand beats, keep the thumb playing its same note *g* (which is common to both chords), and change the upper pair of notes to the pair *a semitone on either side—* below the keynote *c'*, and above the 3rd of the scale, *e'*.

(The chords are described verbally like this to make it easier to find them in other keys, for if you do not know what the notes should be in the key, say, of C sharp, you know what you should *do* to find them.)

(v)   If you master this vigorous waltz-style independent accompaniment, you can ask someone to play the melody (doubled at the octave, using both hands) in a higher register as a duet.

(vi)   Transpose the accompaniment into C sharp, D, B or B flat. (If you know a clarinettist who can play the melody *written* in C, you will have to be able to transpose into B flat, as the clarinet will change the pitch down a tone.)

The songs suggested in this chapter use one pattern throughout a whole piece. The patterns are not childish simplifications but have frequently been used in piano music *and* orchestral music, as the next three pieces show.

7 Cradle Song (Schubert)

(i)   Play the melody. Then landscape it.

(ii)   Sing the melody. Accompany it with a right-hand two-note pattern an 8ve beneath, over bass 5ths for Tonic harmony and an 8ve for Dominant harmony. Once you have established basic harmonies through root-position 5ths, this is often a useful way of smoothing the bass texture:

Ex. 58a

(iii)   Again play the melody, this time over the two-note pattern only, simply observing where it will need modification. You are familiar with the strong simple effect of octave passages: 8ves occurring singly and unexpectedly in a two-part texture are liable to spoil the dialogue, sounding either too strong, in rhythmically weak places, or too naïve; but occasionally they prove effective.

(iv)   Replay, making the desirable modifications of the two-note accompaniment, then write it out.

130

What you have in effect been doing here is working gradually from a root position sketch on Tonic and Dominant to a setting making use of the various inversions of those two chords. In some styles of music this is more appropriate than introducing a wider vocabulary of chords. In the case of the Dominant 7th chord these inversions can be expressed in two-note terms as:

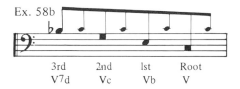

Neither comparative ease of execution nor harmonic usefulness call for them to be necessarily introduced in arithmetical order from 1st to 3rd inversion. It is always encouraging to be able to play something that is immediately *predominantly* successful, which can then be improved or altered in small areas by choice. You will extend your skill by making such small adaptations within this two-note style at moments when the melody and bass together either disturb your ears with a clash or bore you by doubling.

8 Rosamunde (Schubert)

This pattern was also frequently used by classical composers such as Schubert as an accompanimental figure for middle strings (2nd violins and violas) in orchestral and chamber music, or in piano arrangements to take the place of reiterated notes on strings.

131

9 Minuet (Beethoven)

Beethoven, Piano Sonata in G, Op.49, No.2

Tempo di Menuetto

If you treat this Minuet theme by the two-note accompaniment you will be very close to what Beethoven wrote. In the penultimate bar play both notes of the applicable harmony together, but invert their position. Arrange the final bar suitably. Compare your setting with Beethoven (see the Appendix, page 250).

10 John Smith

18th century Scottish

(Introduction)

John Smith, fel - low fine, Can you shoe this horse o' mine? Yes, Sir,

FINE

that I can, Just as well as a - ny man. There's a nail up - on the toe: The

D % al Fine

po - ny then will want to go. There's a nail up - on the heel To make the po-ny scam-per well.

132

In the last song in this chapter, a fourth texture can be found by *combining* the two-note figure with 6ths. The song also shows the value of trying a piece on chords I and V before enlarging the vocabulary of 5ths. For despite the visual message conveyed to many by the melody notes in bar 2, the more restricted vocabulary rings true for such a simple children's song. And an accompaniment so based can effectively convey the scampering pony.

(i)   Play the melody. Landscape with 5ths of I and V.

(ii)   Play the melody over the two-note pattern accompaniment. Note that the harmony in bar 2 may constitute V^9 as in 'Andulko', bar 5.

(iii)   Sing the melody and accompany it with the right-hand two-note pattern over bass 5ths, substituting an octave for all Dominant bars.

(iv)   Replace each second *a* or *b*♭ in the bar in the right-hand part, with the note a 6th above (*f'* or *g'*), returning to the pivot note *c'*, over a bass as in (iii) above. Play the right-hand part staccato to suggest the scampering pony. This is another common accompanimental pattern.

Keep the techniques of this chapter in your repertoire, so that you can use them at will in relevant sections of later pieces in the book. One technique need not last for a whole piece.

If you have studied this chapter in conjunction with Chapter 3, return now to Chapter 4 before continuing these separate accompaniments.

10 MAKING YOUR OWN ACCOMPANIMENTS: II

This chapter is for use in conjunction with **Chapter 4**, and is concerned with the provision of accompaniments to melodies involving the use of all three primary chords, **I, V and IV**, in major keys. In each case the melody should first be landscaped with bass 5ths, so that the harmonic changes are known before a texture is attempted. It should then prove easy to provide, immediately, an accompaniment using one or more of the techniques in **Chapter 9**.

More about Choosing 6ths

In Chapter 9, accompaniments of melodies requiring only chords I and V were served by a vocabulary of the two root bass notes plus four possible 6ths, those beneath the 7th, 8th (or 1st), 2nd and 3rd degrees of the scale. In the key of D:

Play the chords of I and V in this rhythm pattern:

Then add chord IV, to increase the vocabulary to:

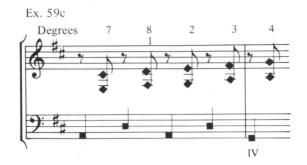

Though it may seem that this vocabulary of 6ths can be extended further, can you hear why this is best avoided?

Chord IV leads happily to the inclusion of I_c (Tonic 2nd inversion), or, in other words, the 'HXB' bass:

So, when you arrange accompaniments in this style, it is not enough merely to ensure that bass and song melody do not move in displeasing parallels between chords IV and V: it is also necessary to keep the ear alert to such parallels between bass notes and right-hand 6ths. Always

136

move from chord IV to chord V with your two hands in opposite directions, like this:

Ex. 59f

This would be a better way of coping with the last two chords in example 59d.

1 Ho-La-Hi
If you cannot remember the tune, turn to page 58.

After landscaping the tune, play an independent accompaniment of bass note and 6th. This song comes from the Tyrolean mountain area and the "Ho-La-Hi" sections would be yodelled. What register might this suggest?

2 Trempe ton pain, Marie

(i)   Landscape, noting where you will use chord IV.

(ii)   Texture for a skipping accompaniment with extended broken chords as in 'Joys Seven' (page 125).

137

3 Punchinello

If you cannot remember the tune, refer to page 70.

(i)   Use an 'oom-pah' texture of bass and 6ths to provide an independent accompaniment.

(ii)   Which is the better 6th to begin with, that below the 1st or 3rd degree of the scale?

(iii)   Did your ear tell you of problems between bars 2 and 3? Here, in context, is the problem solved as in example 59f.

(iv)   How many chords do you need in bar 12? In bar 15?

Keep the rhythmic pattern constant throughout. It seems pointless to change from ♩ ♩ to ♪♪♪♪ in odd bars. So, when the harmonic pace increases, play the left and right hands simultaneously instead of consecutively.

4 Smuggler's Song

If you cannot remember the melody, refer to page 59.

The 'oom-pah' style is only suited to melodies in which the melodic line consistently implies a single harmony over two, three or even four beats. Occasionally, the harmonies of the accompaniment will be even sparser than the landscaping 5ths. You will find the landscaping chords I and V in bars 3 and 15 reduce to a single bass note and 6th. The bass note covers both harmonies, while the 6th, when it arrives, defines the second harmony clearly. In other words, I_c-V is again revealed as fundamentally an appoggiatura over V.

5 Sacramento

If you cannot remember the melody, refer to page 62.

Landscape this song again, then make an accompaniment with the off-beat syncopated rhythm suggested for 'Michael Finnigin' on page 128. See and hear how this affects choices in bars 2 and 3 and at the cadence. What rhythmic patterns will you choose there? After you have decided, consult the Appendix, page 250.

6 Afton Water

Scottish (words by Robert Burns)

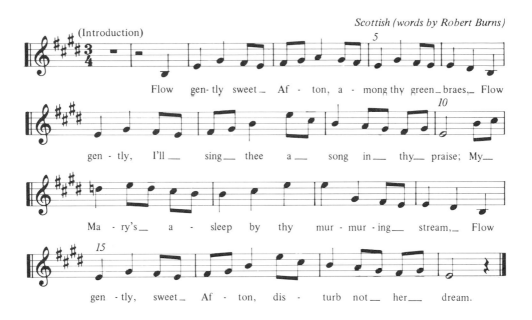

Flow gen-tly sweet _ Af - ton, a - mong thy green _ braes, _ Flow gen - tly, I'll _ sing _ thee a _ song in _ thy _ praise; My _ Ma - ry's _ a - sleep by thy mur - mur - ing _ stream, _ Flow gen - tly, sweet _ Af - ton, dis - turb not _ her _ dream.

You can treat this particularly lovely song on the lines of 'John Smith' (page 132), providing an accompaniment as flowing as the words suggest. Bar 6 is the only tricky one, looking as if it needs several chords. Decide which 5th best serves the first two beats. You can test whether you have found the best choice by playing the root of the chord (together with its octave doubling below) with the sustaining pedal down, and then playing the melody of the whole bar against it. Repeat an 8ve above *and* an 8ve below.

When you have landscaped the song:

(i)   Accompany it with an appropriate two-note pattern.

(ii)   Sing the melody, playing the two-note pattern with your right hand over Tonic 5th and Dominant 8ve where you have landscaped them with your left hand. Link the two-note patterns by step when they change position. Note particularly the part played by the Subdominant.

(iii)   As in 'John Smith', extend the two-note pattern by playing a 6th over the right-hand thumb note on the *second* beat of the bar, and you will have a suitable lyrical accompaniment.

(iv)   Try to find a few more refinements from your repertoire of patterns, such as 'HXB' bass (which may become an effective 'HX' only, at Imperfect Cadences).

7 Waltzing Matilda

19th century Australian

Imagine that you are going to accompany a solo violin or flute, and that your accompaniment can also be played by a group of strings. The melody will sound better in a register an 8ve higher, so try to hear it there.

There are some problems in harmonic pacing, which may require two harmonies in some bars but only one in others. The harmonic pace of 'Punchinello' tended to speed up at cadences: here you have the reverse.

In setting any piece, there is a natural tendency to continue at a faster pace of harmonic change once you have started: this leads to problems in bars 11 and 12. Here, two harmonies are suggested by 5th landscaping but not when the accompanying 6th comes with the pair of semiquavers in bar 11. If you find a one-bar harmonic pace right for this phrase, you may feel that bars 2 and 3 need some cadential structure.

Further Songs Needing All Three Primary Chords

Camptown Races (see page 23).
Oh, Susanna
John Brown's Body (see page 68).
The Cuckoo
The Grand Old Duke of York

11 MAKING YOUR OWN ACCOMPANIMENTS: III

This chapter is concerned with making accompaniments to some of the modal songs landscaped in Chapter 5. More aural judgement and skill are required, because in modal music you have a wider repertoire of chords to choose from. So the essential prior landscaping must be valid and be remembered, when the simple 5ths are replaced by a fuller pattern of accompaniment. The wider the choice, the greater the scope for error.

During the centuries when European music was modal, religious choral music developed ahead of instrumental music. There was as yet no orchestra, as we understand the term: and at first much written music—what is known as 'art music' as opposed to 'folk' music (though folk music is in no way inherently less 'artistic')—was largely based on choral textures. A set of pieces might be headed 'for voices or viols'. So styles of independent accompaniment, as opposed to close harmonisation of a melody, are less applicable to modal 'art music' than to most kinds of diatonic music.

However, folk songs were largely unharmonised and unaccompanied; or accompanied by instruments such as the Celtic harp. Rippling up notes of a chord, for that reason designated *arpeggiando*, was a style of playing commonly used in harp accompaniments. We shall make use of this.

The bass-note-plus-6th pattern of accompaniment should only be used in contexts where it really sounds appropriate. But of course the 6th can be arranged in various ways and need not always suggest typical staccato 'oom-pah'.

1 What shall we do with the Drunken Sailor?
If you cannot remember the melody, refer to page 76.

This is a modal sea shanty. A lively 'oom-pah' accompaniment is certainly appropriate here. There are various ways of arranging this, having regard both to speed/pace considerations and to choice of harmonies.

(i)   The whole song can be done on two chords only. Which two? Landscape it that way. Then arrange an independent accompaniment of bass note and 6th.

Whereas the parallel lurchings of neighbouring chords D minor and C major (chords I and VII of the mode) are acceptable with landscaping 5ths in so primitive a modal song, an accompaniment arranged so:

Ex. 60

is surely too ugly to be acceptable. Can you improve on this? Try using the other 6th which expresses the chord of C major? Why is this preferable?

(ii)   Now investigate the other three landscaping possibilities for the interesting cadence bars 7–8 and texture them in terms of a 6ths accompaniment. One involves another *single* harmony in bar 7: two involve *pairs* of the principal modal chords in that bar. When you use two chords in the bar, how will you arrange then rhythmically?

(iii)   With regard to pace, you have probably been playing alternating crotchet beats, as above. Should you want the song to go faster, will you put more into the accompaniment or less?

In view of the fact that one harmony covers a pair of bars for most of the song, this pair can be treated as a single unit by tying the second bass note back to the first (see page 128), producing the syncopated rhythm used in a number of previous songs. This makes the song considerably more inebriate! How does this change of pace affect the choices at the cadence? For examples, see the Appendix, page 251.

2 The Oak and the Ash

If you cannot remember the melody, refer to page 81.

(i)   Landscape

(ii)   Make a 'Harp-style' accompaniment by using the landscaping chords, enriched by being filled out and spread in a leisurely upwards *arpeggiando*:

Ex. 62a

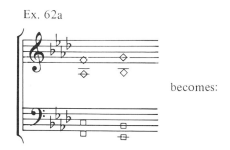

becomes:

Ex. 62b

A   north coun-try maid up to   Lon - don had strayed,

etc.

The chords can be further expanded; for even in major chords the doubled 3rd will be perfectly acceptable, because the spacing is that of the harmonic series. Play the first chord a 3rd higher, in C, then look again at the series (page vi).

Ex. 62c

3 Greensleeves

If you cannot remember the melody, refer to page 79.

This is one of the most rewarding of the modal songs to accompany. In Chapter 5 it was found that harmonic landscaping with one 5th per bar would accommodate all familiar variants of the melody:

Ex. 61

I   VII   I   V V

(i)   Without playing the tune, make an accompaniment with bass note and right-hand 6th. The melodic variants occurring on the semiquavers, being decorative mordents, will still be open to choice without affecting the accompaniment. But this time you will have to decide which version of the 7th degree is going to be sung in bars 4 and 7 and form the accompanying 6th accordingly: for the 3rd of the chord will be one of the notes of that 6th and will define the variable Dominant as minor or major. You also have another choice to make at the end: Tierce de Picardie or not? (See page 80.)

(ii)   Here are four possible accompanying patterns of 6ths:

Ex. 61a

etc.

Ex. 61b

etc.

Ex. 61c

Ex. 61d

The laborious 'oom-pah' of (a) provides an inadequate texture for the lyrical sway of this melody. To play it twice per bar as in (b) is somewhat jerky and fails to enhance the differing dotted rhythm of each second beat—which should be felt to lead on to each next bar (a reason why two harmonies per bar may be found less pleasing than one). However, to combine (a) and (b) to make (c) allows the second beat pattern to float, with its lilting mordent, like a slender bridge to the next bar: and if you texture it lightly by breaking up the 6th into two solo notes, phrased as in (d) it makes a specially good 'lay-out' (as it is called) of the component notes of each harmony and provides a suitable texture for this lyrical melody. Of course you will still need two harmonies in bar 7, arranged as at (b).

(iii)   An accompaniment based on landscaping using two different 5ths per bar (except at phrase endings) will need to be played as in example 61b, and may be found acceptable with the added richness of harmonies. (See the Appendix, page 241.)

4 God Rest You Merry, Gentlemen

English Carol

The true modal character of this folk carol has been obscured by hymnal settings that plod along in stodgy crotchets, weighing down the pace and destroying the rhythmic flow of the melody as well as the original tonality. The pace should be a minim walk.

(i)   Landscape with only one 5th per bar, except where two seem essential. Do not be content with three bars of the same harmony in the first phrase. If you find bar 14 a problem, consider the first melody note as a suspension forming an accented passing note. Heard like this, which melody note will indicate the harmony?

(ii)   Imagine you are playing a harp and imitate the rippled chords on the piano as you sing the melody.

A similar *arpeggiando* style was used to accompany the *recitative* sections (in which the drama of the story was declaimed or 'recited') in the operas and oratorios of the seventeenth and eighteenth centuries. These accompaniments were extemporised on a given chordal basis on the *harp*sichord. Here is a famous example from Purcell's *Dido and Aeneas*:

146

Ex 63

Thy hand, Be - lin - da! dark - - - - - - ness

shades me, On thy bo - som let me rest.

5 The Animals Went in Two by Two
If you cannot remember the melody, refer to page 18.

A lively contrast to the previous pair of songs, this is again well suited to an 'oom-pah' accompaniment. It is most important to hear that the harmonies you choose for bars 9 to 14 bring out the logical construction of these phrases.

(i)   Landscape the song again. Then see if you have remembered the sounds of bars 9 to 14 correctly, by looking again at the Appendix, page 243.

(ii)   Arrange the harmonies as an independent accompaniment of bass note followed by 6th, at a good marching pace. After you have done this, read the Appendix, page 251.

(iii)   Play the accompaniment in another key.

6 Four English Country Dances

These tunes should be played lightly and vigorously at a springy pace. In each case landscape first. Then break up the chord over the span of its operation. The last part of the bar is often best served by a rest, as in 'Greensleeves'. In one case, simply to play the chords spread *arpeggiando*, with a good accent, is exactly what Cecil Sharp did in his famous settings of these dances. In another he used only the 5th in a drum rhythm for the first section of the dance, as you did with the French dance 'Mattachins' in Chapter 7. Simplicity may again be a virtue.

(i)　**Goddesses**

(ii)　**Gooseberry Blossoms**

(iii) **Nonesuch**

After you have made your accompaniment, look at Cecil Sharp's setting in the Appendix, page 252.

(iv) You may now like to try an independent accompaniment for 'Dargason', which you first met in Chapter 5, page 86.

Composing an Accompaniment

The simple musical devices advocated in these last three chapters enable a player to extemporise an arrangement quickly, often by the use of a single musical pattern throughout a piece. Using them, many players will produce virtually identical settings. A composed arrangement is a more individual thing, taking more time and thought to construct. The following independent accompaniment illustrates how a composer might build a simple accompaniment using the same processes. Play it and study it.

7 O Rare Turpin

150

(i)　Λ framework of rhythm alone for the song would require sounds on 1st and 4th beats. The harmonic changes occur on 1st and 3rd beats. Notice how both needs have been satisfied in the setting.

(ii)　The accompaniment is built on a bass note plus 6th arrangement of the landscaping harmonies, the 6th filled out with another note of the chord (full-sized notes) and by passing notes (small notes). In the third phrase the chord is expanded, using both available 6ths (in terms of the way you have been working, marked by dotted lines).

(iii)　What chord of the mode is that on (a) the first beat of bar 8? and (b) the second beat of bar 12? Notice how the conviction carried by an essential harmony, in broken form, renders component notes of such a chord acceptable even when they clash with next-door passing notes in the melody (melody c'' with harmony $d^{b'}$ in bar 8, melody $a^{b'}$ with harmony g' in bar 12). Do these disturb you? Such coinciding notes may need checking in performance, to hear if they are acceptable; and acceptability may to some extent depend on good phrasing, balance of tone and accentuation in playing and singing.

If this chapter has been studied in conjunction with Chapter 5, it is essential to return to Chapter 6 before continuing here.

12 MAKING YOUR OWN ACCOMPANIMENTS: IV

This chapter is for use in conjunction with Chapter 6 on Minor harmonisation.

1 Czech Folk Song
If you cannot remember the melody, refer to page 96.

(i)   Before you embark on an accompaniment there is one improvement that may be added to landscaping. Like so many pieces, this is a miniature version of sonata form. The first phrase is in the tonic minor key, the second in the relative major. The third is in the nature of a tiny development section, with one two-bar phrase in that second key, repeated sequentially in the original key. The last phrase is a recapitulation in the original key. This means that, proportionately, most of the second half of the piece is in the 'home' key. After you have landscaped the sequential phrase in bars 11–12, what could you do at the beginning of the recapitulation to lessen the certainty that the piece has already arrived back in the home key? Experiment with this, for the present only in terms of 5ths.

(ii)   Had you been dealing with a cadence, what kind of cadence would postpone the sense of home-coming at bar 13? The connection between the end of the penultimate and the beginning of the final phrase can be solved in terms of that cadence, regarded as a bridge between the two phrases.
Remember to seek alternative chords in a systematic manner. After you have decided, see the Appendix, page 253.

(iii)   An 'oom-pah' accompaniment suits this melody so well that it was probably used from the time the song began. Which bars seem particularly to support this assumption? Convert the landscaping of the whole piece into an independent accompaniment of single bass note and right-hand 6th. Notice and remember that the change of harmony in bar 13 from I to VI conveniently involves *the same right-hand 6th* (f' and a^b).

153

(iv)   Now add the relevant extra note *within* each 6th, so that you have 3-note right-hand chords (which will not now be of identical shape). This will define the harmony more completely, although it is already defined by bass and 6ths alone. The extra notes only give more body to the texture.

(v)   List the chords you are using: you are using chords on nearly every degree of the minor scale. Now play the accompaniment starting on all possible keynotes. You will then have played in *every* minor key *and* its relative major. This is easier than you imagine and will increase your confidence in finding your way about the keyboard without notation.

From Landscaping to Counterpoint

Playing a dance on your own, you will have to incorporate the melody with the accompaniment, as in the Cecil Sharp setting of 'Nonesuch' on page 252. But in more sophisticated concert music such as the 18th-century suites of dances, melodies often had almost equally melodious basses.

A most useful tool to use in making such a 'counterpoint' is the following three-note 'motif'. A motif relates to a melody as a cell seen under a microscope does to a living organ: it is the smallest recognisable particle.

(i)   Play up the first 3 notes of the scale of C major, as a triplet. Repeat this in ascending sequence rising, one degree at a time, until you circle

round the upper key-note and rest on it:

Double the whole at the 8ve, with the left hand.

(ii)   Reverse the three notes, mirror-wise, with the left hand an 8ve lower and combine that inversion with the right-hand part (as it was before), both hands progressing in ascending sequence.

(iii)   Reverse the parts (right-hand degrees 3, 2, 1, left-hand 1, 2, 3) and return to middle *c'* in descending sequence. It is most important that the

pattern is seen *mirror-wise* in the mind: as

because to think merely of contrary motion can change the harmony,

from C major to A minor:

154

2 Bourrée

(i)   Landscape this dance from Chapter 6 again, using these places for 5ths:

Ex. 65

Bass 5ths

(ii)   Playing single bass notes (the bottom notes only of the 5ths), use the framework of this single-line bass to introduce 'mirror' contrary-motion 'counterpoint' as you have studied it above, where you hear scope for it. Make sure that it expresses the same harmonies as the landscaping. If there is a passage where use of the mirror bass may *look* appropriate but does not *sound* so, return to 5ths or single bass notes alone, in a suitable register.

As at the end of the Czech tune, you may have found that a 1st inversion of Tonic (*c* in the bass) leads best into the cadence (*c*, *d*, *e*, A). The 'HXB' idiom (with or without the 'X') has now become expanded by *two* antecedents. This very common cadential bass should be established as a new unit in your harmonic vocabulary.

(iii)   After completion, play the left-hand part alone. Consider whether it makes a good bass line, with a sense of purpose and some melodic content of its own. If so, it should be possible for two instruments such as violin and cello to play it happily as a duet.

(iv)   This slender texture can be given more body. At each rhythmic point *where the original landscaping 5th stood*, add a single extra note with the right hand, to complete the harmony. This 'middle' note will be held for the length of that basic chord, unless broken for phrasing reasons. Here is a possible bar 3, showing all the three processes:

155

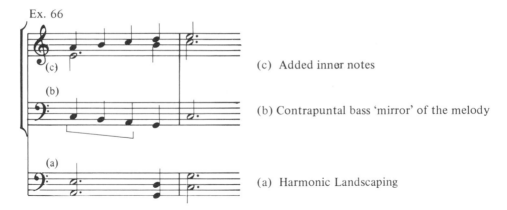

Ex. 66

(c) Added inner notes

(b) Contrapuntal bass 'mirror' of the melody

(a) Harmonic Landscaping

If players are available, write out this score and parts for string trio. You may find it an improvement to change the register of some middle notes, such as the last two in the passage above.

3 Gavotte

If you cannot remember the melody, refer to page 97.

(i)   After landscaping apply treatments (ii) and (iii) as for the Bourrée (page 155). If your bass counterpoint is good you may not necessarily want to add any notes between the parts—or you may add them in some sections only. '

(ii)   In such a contrapuntal texture it is acceptable to accompany the half-bar anacrusis, so long as quality of touch maintains the essential rhythmic shaping of 'light, light, strong'. That is reinforced here by arrival at the root position on the strong beat:

Ex. 67

Continue the bass descent, selecting preferred inflections of the 7th and 6th degrees.

At the end of the first phrase a further quaver passing-note will link into an obvious procedure for the second phrase. After completion, compare your setting with that given in the Appendix, page 253, which shows the close relationship between the continuous linear counterpoint and the landscaping 5ths. The 5ths may be likened to a tailor's paper pattern, pinned to the cloth at the outset but later removed from the finished garment, which is nevertheless much the better for its application in the first place.

Working this way means that each stage is musically valid: and that the clarity of texture at each stage enables you to hear very clearly what you are doing. So with each sketch you can 'touch in' the details further, on a secure basis.

(iii)   Landscape again the first Bach Gavotte (see page 98). Consult Bach's original, which is available in many editions, and study how *his* counterpoint relates to *your* landscaping.

If this chapter has been studied in conjunction with Chapter 6, return now to Chapter 7.

13 MAKING YOUR OWN ACCOMPANIMENTS: V

Three different tonalities have now been landscaped and textured on their respective principal chords. In terms of the seven white notes on the keyboard (their relationships being the same when transposed) the chords you have used are:

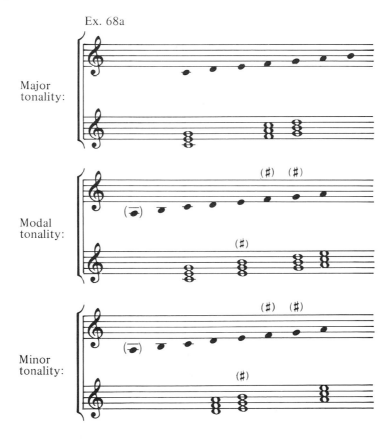

Add all these together:

And the total is only six different chords!

It is amazing that such a wide variety of music can be produced with such a minute vocabulary of chords. For practical purposes a vital conclusion must be drawn from this fact: *the chords you select and the order of succession in which you combine them are exceedingly important.* They either establish the tonality of a given melody, or, if ill-chosen, create a piece in which the tonality is confused, 'neither fish nor fowl'.

Now consider all those six chords in the context of C major. (Minor chords are shown small.)

Ex. 68b

You will see that the three primary chords are the *only* major chords and must therefore be responsible for establishing the overall impression of major tonality. Students already familiar with all six chords in major keys know the three minor ones as 'secondary triads'. What is the other possible function of these three chords?

It is vital to remember that secondary chords of one key are also primary chords of another key. In each diatonic tonality, primary and secondary chords are of opposite character.

> *In a major key*, the three primary chords are major, the three secondary chords minor.
> *In a minor key*, the three primary chords are minor, the three secondary chords major.

Through studying modal harmonisation, with its mixture of minor and major *principal* chords, you have followed the evolution to diatonic minor harmony with its clearly defined *areas* of minor and major tonality. The great majority of minor melodies contains sections in the relative major. Therefore all six of the chords have been used in harmonising minor music. The use of secondary chords in minor harmonisation presents no problem if you confine major chords to those areas where there is modulation to the relative major. Then, they become, in effect, primaries of that key. But if they are haphazardly juxtaposed, the tonality conveyed by player to listener will be modal, not diatonic minor.

In major music, modulation to the relative minor is not so important. A vast number of major melodies contain no modulation: and when modulation does occur, the most likely key is that of the Dominant, another major. In major music, secondary chords may well be used to fulfil their role of *secondary importance*, but they must *not* be grouped together because they are the *same chords* as the primaries of the related minor tonality and if allowed to predominate in any area they will establish a minor key and—whatever you may have intended—become minor primaries. To retain major tonality, the minor secondary chords must be used sparsely and linked to the major primaries to allow that major tonality to remain undisputed. Otherwise the tonality may become translated to modal, or simply become 'fish-and-fowl'.

For a Teacher's note on the chord on the 7th degree see the Appendix, page 254.

1 Anna Marie
If you cannot remember the melody, refer to page 46.

(i)　Landscape on the 5ths of chords I and V only.

(ii)　Play an independent accompaniment of bass note and 6th on those harmonies, arranged in a suitable rhythm.

(iii)　Where do you feel you might like a contrast of harmonic colour in this piece? In your previous setting the chorus involved the same harmonies as the verse, in slightly different order. You will notice that whereas the two melodic phrases of the verse are identical, the two phrases of the chorus are different but similar, having a distinct rhyming quality, something even stronger than the sequence. But for the earlier restriction to use chords I and V only, you might have included chord IV. Try this in the chorus and see if it helps to rhyme the two phrases.

(iv)　Play bars 5 and 6 over bars 7 and 8 simultaneously, as the bars appear on the page, one above the other. What does this reveal? Whereas sequences one degree above or below will obviously require different harmonies, sequences a 3rd away may share the same harmonies—as indeed they did, in this case, when set by chords I and V only. But although chord IV may fit the c'' in the first phrase, it does not create the same sound effect in the second phrase.

(v)　Try adding some 'secondary' chords. Because the principal modal chords lie a 3rd away from each other, particular care has to be taken in deciding which of two chords to use. And this carries over into minor harmonisation where, if the implications of a melody are not carefully listened to *before* a left-hand part is added, it is only too easy to retain minor harmonies in a passage which ought to have been treated in the relative major. Using this same care in major music, alternative harmonies may be judiciously introduced to make a more varied arrangement, *after* landscaping in primary 5ths. But these 'secondary' chords—the three minor chords on 2nd, 3rd and 6th degrees of any major scale—are, of course, also the primaries of its relative minor key and need to be used with discretion. Indiscriminately interspersed with major primaries, they can easily convert the sound to a modal tonality ... or make nonsense.

(vi)   In the chorus of 'Anna Marie', as the inversion of any 3rd is a 6th, accompanimental 6ths will follow the melody of both lines at the same time, line 1 beneath and line 2 above:

Ex. 69a

There is now the option, as a second thought, to treat the first-beat notes—*b'* and *g'*—and the second beat—*c''* and *a'*—as:

Ex. 69b   Ex. 69c

and

There is no need to sketch these alternatives in 5ths, which should be reserved for landscaping. Simply give the same 6th a different bass note, adopting the latter in each case:

Ex. 69d

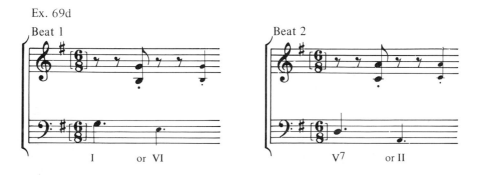

(vii)   What effect will secondary chords have if you use them throughout the first phrase like this?

Ex. 69e

It is imperative to return to the original diatonic primary chords for each second bar, to maintain the major tonality of the whole.

(viii) The accompaniment of VI-II, V-I now fits both phrases equally. It brings out their rhyming quality and distinguishes the chorus from the verse. As a further refinement, the four-fold repetition of this chorus phrase may be relieved by using a dropping bass and a rising bass for alternate phrases:

Ex. 69f

with the right-hand 6ths bouncing in above on each third quaver.

2 Green and White

If you cannot remember the melody, refer to page 43.

(i)   Landscape on I and V.

(ii)   Play an accompaniment of bass note and 6th on those harmonies.

(iii)   Enrich this accompaniment with secondary chords, where you think fit, by altering bass notes only. Subsequently you might like to approach the first changed harmony by a quaver passing note in the bass. Do you find it preferable to change the harmonies in the repeated phrase, or in the different phrase? (For a further Teacher's note on secondary chords, see the Appendix, page 254.)

3 Cader Idris

Welsh

(i)   After you have played the melody through, see if you can play a waltz-style accompaniment straight away, by summing up the harmonies defined or implied by each bar of melody. Sing the tune, or get another player to play the melody, as a duet. Listen carefully to make sure that what you are playing fits with each beat of the melody. The right hand may play in 6ths or in three-note chords. Play the first bar of the accompaniment twice as an introduction. After you have completed this, see how many of the following points you have discovered for yourself:

(a)   In a waltz, it is easy to settle down complacently into repeating identical second and third beats and then to be caught out when they need to change. In which bars is this so?

(b)   It is natural at first to retain chord I for bar 2; but this may lead to parallel movement between chords I and II. There are two ways to avoid this. Either alter the chord in bar 2, so that an intervening chord separates the two adjacent chords: or retain chord I and invert chord II to II_b in bar 3, so avoiding parallel movement of adjacent chords.

164

(c)   The best chord for bar 19 may not be the one most apparent to the eye; but notice that the first and last notes may be used as clues to the ear.

(d)   In bar 23, you may like to use more than one bass note.

(e)   On the last beat of bar 24, if you add, with the left thumb, the vital note to turn that new key chord *back* into the Dominant 7th of the old key, it will link nicely into the recapitulation.

(ii)   Re-texture the accompaniment in a smooth and flowing broken-chord style, beginning:

4 The Ash Grove

Apply similar treatments to this song. after landscaping it.

(i)   Waltz accompaniment.

(ii)   Flowing broken-chord accompaniment built on those harmonies.

(iii) Enrich, on the repeat of the first complete phrase, by introducing passing-notes in the bass on third beats, where appropriate.

(iv)   Try using a 'mirror' technique. This will not be scalic, but contrary motion over the interval of a 3rd, between song melody and bass, as in:

This is useful on many occasions, especially over the chord of II. It involves an alternation of root and 1st inversion, but is best thought of as melodic counterpoint between treble and bass. In how many bars could you use this 'mirror' technique?

PART III

14 ENRICHING THE TEXTURE: II

The process to be studied next enables the player to produce what is commonly called 'full harmony': that is, a faster pace of harmonic change than was possible when using 5ths in the bass. For 5ths prescribe root positions of chords, which are too strong to allow music to flow if they are used in close succession. It is still essential to think horizontally and to consider stretches of melody at a time, never hindering the musical flow to build-up individual chords vertically unless, like a dentist finding an occasional cavity or rotten tooth which needs investigation in detail, you locate the odd displeasing sound which does not match the aural pattern you expected to hear. The critical attention of the ear is essential: it must always act as watchdog, taking over the role of teacher and building up your competence and confidence. As you learn to *ask yourself the right questions* you will learn to find your own way to good solutions.

1 This Old Man
If you cannot remember the melody, refer to page 30.

> This old man, he played one,
> He played nick-nack on my drum.
> Nick-nack paddy whack, give a dog a bone;
> This old man came rolling home.

(i)   Play the melody in the key of F.

(ii)   Accompany it with a left-hand Tonic 5th *only*, played at a suitable register and in a rhythmic figure throughout which speeds the lively melody on its way, but does not clutter it. See the Appendix, page 254, 1(ii).

(iii)   Leave that rhythmic pattern on one side for the moment, and concentrate on finding the right Primary 5ths where changes of harmony are desirable. Keep the pace of harmonic change sparse, with not more

167

than one left-hand 5th per bar. Then replace your rhythmic pattern, applying it to these Primary 5ths. See the Appendix, page 255, 1(iii).

You have now treated this melody in terms of the sketch process used in Part I and produced an arrangement which carries conviction, because the style is consistent and it is easy to play up to speed. Continue by treating it in terms of Part II.

(iv)   Double *every* melody note by a 3rd or a 6th beneath it, played by the right hand. Stick to one or other interval throughout. Then decide which is most satisfactory, or whether in some areas the choice is equal.

Should you at any point find neither interval satisfactory, or practicable at the necessary speed, remember that the quickest way out of a problem is to go back to a simpler process. In this case omit the 3rd or 6th and revert to a unison, until the previous interval proves satisfactory again. Put it in again as soon as you can. Singing the lower part can help you find how soon.

(v)   Play the above arrangement with your right hand and add the previously selected Primary 5ths, one per bar, with your left hand. Do they combine satisfactorily? Which upper interval proved generally the more satisfactory, 3rds or 6ths?

(vi)   Play your right-hand part alone again, only departing from the prevalent interval at the few places where a unison is preferable; but this time play the lower line of it with your *left* hand. Sing that lower line too, thinking of it as a part for alto voice, second violin or the lower of a pair of recorders.

(vii)   Now drop the left-hand part to the register an octave lower, so that the two lines become a tenth apart. The unison in bars 5–6 will now become an octave. You may also wish to change the last two lower notes to strengthen the bass part at the end, indicating a perfect cadence from *note to note* within the final bar, instead of from bar to bar (bars 7–8) as in (iii) and (v) above. How satisfying do you find this version? Does it imply a fuller harmonisation lying within these two parts?

Now take the first four bars only:

(viii) Play the first 10th, right hand c'' and left hand a. What chord does this suggest? What is the missing note? Add that note, playing it with your right-hand thumb.

(ix)   Play the first four bars only, with melody and bass lines a 10th apart, repeating that same 'thumb-note' within each 10th for as long as it proves satisfactory, then find another thumb-note that can also be repeated effectively for as long as possible.

You will find that your two parallel horizontal lines have been transformed into what is commonly known as 'full harmony', consisting of a rapid sequence of vertical chords which, after the initial one, you never had to think of individually. Following a simple process which, once mastered, you can apply on your own in a myriad other contexts, you have *experienced the music before analysing it theoretically*. This is the best and the most pleasing way to learn. However, do not accept the result without critical listening. Students working in a group should each play a version, the others commenting on it. Does anything need to be altered? Is there anything to which the musical 'dentist' should attend?

If a problem arises on the third quaver of bar 3, at the syllable "nick-", can you describe in what way the sound at that moment is *not* what you expected to hear? The solution is always to thin the texture again, back to the simple 10th, so that you can analyse the character of harmony it seems to imply. For if a sound strikes you as wrong, that shows that you have a conception of a right sound in your imaginative ear. Listen to the 10th at that third quaver and ask yourself how you hear the harmony implied at that moment. Is it major or minor?

Ex. 72a

Your answer to that question should enable you to make your own correction (provided you remember what key you are in!). When you have decided, check with the Appendix, page 255, 1(ix). Replay the first four bars: how many different notes have you played with your right thumb? What degrees of the scale are they? Noting these degrees will make it easier to play these first four bars in any key.

(x) Now slow down the pace as you play, so that you can analyse by ear and then name the chords on each quaver beat. (Remember that the shorthand label for the 1st inversion of the Dominant 7th is $V^7{}_b$, and for the second inversion $V^7{}_c$.) You will realise that you could not even name them numerically, let alone build each one up vertically, at the speed at which you have been able to *play* this beautifully dove-tailed sequence of chords in root positions and various inversions by the horizontal process of treble and bass a 10th apart, with sparse repeated or sustained thumb-notes between (first and fifth degrees of the key in this case).

If you kept f' as your thumb-note throughout bar 3 it will have sounded quite satisfactory played fast. But it may now present a difficulty when you try to analyse the chord on the third quaver. If you play it slowly in isolation, you will hear that the f' wants to drop to e':

Ex. 72b

This reveals f' as a suspension and shows e' to be the indigenous note; so the e' defines the third quaver chord as V^7_c (with the root only implied, as it was by the alternative thumb-note suggested in the Appendix). But to play e' for that one quaver involves too frequent changes of thumb-note to be recommended to those embarking on this 3rds bass technique, particularly when you play the sequence in other keys:

Ex. 72c

thumb

Therefore students are strongly advised at this stage to use only the *two* thumb-notes, tonic and dominant. The f' changes to c' half way through bar 3 for the rest of the phrase, as that fifth degree of the scale is common to both Tonic and Dominant chords. Equally the keynote, until the change, is common to both Tonic and Subdominant chords. If you play bar 3 again slowly, with the thumb-note d' on the third quaver—a natural thing to do since you have been practising right-hand 6ths above primary 5ths—you should now realise what happens when you add 6ths to a 3rd or 10ths bass arrangement, and appreciate the need to keep thumb-notes stationary wherever possible.

(xi) Play these first four bars in the 3rds bass arrangement, while another student plays the original landscaping 5ths underneath, in duet. The enriched version, with its fuller texture and faster pace of harmonic change still rests on the same harmonies at the principal rhythmic points (the beginning of each bar) vindicating again the concept of harmonic landscaping (see the Appendix page 255, 1(xi)). You have, as it were, sketched this tune in charcoal, in watercolours and in oils, and you can choose the version best suited to any particular circumstance.

(xii) Play the 3rds bass setting in F minor and you will find the technique equally valid.

(xiii) Play these first four bars in *every* major key, following the hand pattern. You will easily be able to hear and correct any errors, which will only involve occasional dentistry amongst a predominantly good set of teeth! This task conscientiously performed will establish a manual mastery of the basic technique.

Now treat the last four bars

(xiv) Recall that:

    (a)   using 3rds and 6ths above primary 5ths, 3rds were generally more satisfactory.

    (b)   in your first sketch you found unisons better than 3rds in bars 5 and 6 (example 72d here) and this, in turn, gave you 10ths when you dropped the left hand an octave (example 72e). Yet again, a simpler alternative for these two bars will provide a musical contrast before you return to 3rds over 5ths up to the cadence.

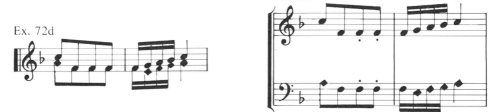

Ex. 72d

Ex. 72e

This doubling back from keynote to leading note in the under part of bar 6 may seem a small occurrence, singular to this particular tune. But in fact it will crop up frequently in the work ahead; so it should be imprinted on mental and manual memory *now*, in its simplest form. Play bar 6 in several different registers. Repeat in the Dominant key.

(xv) There are various possibilities at the final cadence:

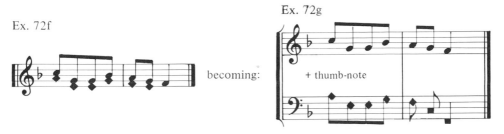

Ex. 72f

Ex. 72g

becoming:

+ thumb-note

Find one thumb-note that can be repeated or sustained for the first five quavers.

(xvi) Follow the 6th your right hand has produced in the last bar with successive 6ths. Play the last two bars slowly: analyse and name the chords produced at each quaver beat. In the penultimate bar, you may think the 3rds bass sounds rather contrived and the move from I_b to V_b too jerky. If you go back to the original landscaping in primary 5ths and take the *c* bass for the whole bar in the left hand and play example 72f above it, you may feel this more musical. Beware, as you learn more elaborate handling, of putting ingenuity before musical judgement. It is only too easy to do. Now play the whole song through in your final arrangement. Try to play it in several different keys.

2 The Harmonic Series

Your earliest setting of melodies (as in 'Papa a du Tabac') often involved the combination of the *second and third* or *second and fourth* octaves of the harmonic series, *i.e.* a more or less scalic melody over a 5th two octaves below. Subsequent settings over bass 5ths combined the *second and third* octaves. Example 73 suggests how the 10ths bass derives naturally out of a combination of the *third and fourth* octaves of the series.

(i) Add a middle thumb-note to the two lines written in the treble clef. The note *c"* could be used throughout; but you may prefer *f"* under the *d'''* (the highest note) and 6ths under the last two upper notes.

(ii) Add passing notes in the left hand to make a line of continuous 10ths, except for the 'cadence' at the end. The relationship to 'This Old Man' with 10ths bass is clear if you play from the highest note, with the *f"* thumb-note just to start with.

172

(iii)   By playing *all* the notes as they are written in example 73, combined, you can demonstrate more clearly than ever that sparsely-placed 5ths may underpin a faster pace of harmonic enrichment. Press the sustaining pedal and play the three bass stave notes heavily: while that sound stays, play the three-part version with c'' throughout on the treble stave. Even the $b^{\flat}{}''$ and the $b^{\natural}{}''$ will be heard quite 'harmoniously', as they are part of the harmonic series. By listening to this very carefully, you will find pedalling decisions easier to take where they are not specific in much piano music.

3 Summing Up

The four new discoveries in this chapter become generalisations for application in the future. Revise them again before you proceed:

(a)   How to turn a two-part arrangement of parallel 10ths into 3rd bass harmony by inserting a prevalent 'thumb-note'.

(b)   How to verify the validity of the 3rds bass process by studying a spread-out diagram of the third and fourth octaves of the harmonic series. When this area is made use of for both melody and bass, a faster pace of harmonic texturing is achieved, which lies above one or more 'landscaping' 5ths, which may be stated or discarded. The most used thumb-note is found to be the 5th degree of the scale, the *dominant* note. This confirms the discovery in Chapter 3, that the harmonic series reveals the dominant 7th chord (defined in its third octave) and this in turn reveals the dominant thumb-note to be the same note as the 'fundamental' of the series: and, like the fundamental, the thumb-note moves at a slower pace and 'binds' the faster-moving changes together into a coherent texture.

(c)   How, because the 3rd below the keynote implies minor (secondary) harmony, it may be necessary to use an octave bass under the keynote, which can soon 'double back' to the leading note into 3rds bass again.

(d)   How you may need to revert to the *earlier process* of 6ths over a cadential bass at the end of a piece, or section.

15 THIN AND FAST, OR THICK AND SLOW?

1 Down in Demerara
If you cannot remember the melody, refer to page 22.

Leaving the anacrusic *d'* unaccompanied:

(i)   Repeat the thumb-note on every crotchet pulse, establishing a brisk marching pace, over 3rds bass.

(ii)   This time alter the pace, adapting the setting as though to play for small children running, at the crisp trotting speed the sick horse is unable to do! Do this by playing the reiterated dominant *d'* thumb-notes *after* each crotchet, instead of on each beat, providing a continuous staccato quaver movement. The left-hand part may be either staccato or legato, the two parts at close register or more widely separated. When the right-hand part changes to 6ths at cadences, break them up to maintain the quaver movement. Although a change of thinking is involved for the performer, from 3rds bass to cadential, no break is apparent in the texture as the two dovetail so neatly:

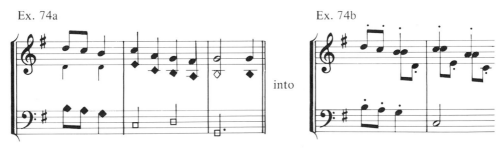

Ex. 74a   Ex. 74b

into

(iii)   Play both styles of arrangement in the tonic minor key (G minor) as well.

(iv)   Look again at the 'two-note' accompaniment figure on page 126, 'Sur le Pont d'Avignon', which pivots round an off-beat dominant. It could be considered for any melody based on chords I and V only as, viewed vertically, the chords are alternations of I_b and $V^7{}_d$. In choosing a natural pace for *singing* this song, it will probably prove more suitable to the words than a 3rds bass harmonisation which, even if played with a strong first beat accent, provides a one-beat harmonic pace, according to the crotchets of this notation. Indeed, the song might more appropriately be written:

Ex. 74c

There was a man who had a hors-e-lum

comparing closely with 'Michael Finnigin' (page 38). Remind yourself that *pitch notation* is absolute, but *rhythmic notation* is only relative (see page 27, viii), and that sensitive musical judgment must be used in its interpretation.

Not only will two pulses to the bar better match the verbal rhythm of this song, but a duple interpretation is also better suited pitch-wise when it comes to pacing the two-note accompanimental figure. Compare examples 74d and 74e here:

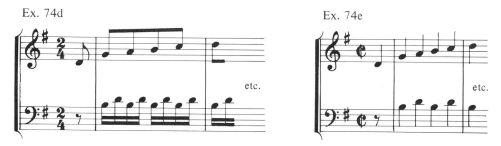

Ex. 74d

Ex. 74e

The slower pattern matches one chord to each note of an ascending scale:

Ex. 74f

I V I V   I

This shows that in *any* scalic melody running up or down degrees 1–5, *alternate* notes belong to chord I and *alternate* ones chord V (with degree 5 common to both chords). This is why the extended broken chord also fits scalic melodies (see page 126). So the appropriate pace for 'two-note' figure here is:

175

Ex. 74g

There was a man who had a hors-e-lum, had a hors-e-lum

When asked for a flowing accompaniment, students too often suggest an 'Alberti' bass, a choice probably due to the conception of chords as essentially close position triads. You will understand why this often proves disastrous, for the wrong notes of the chord coincide:

Ex. 74h

The Alberti bass is in fact quite difficult to use, its success depending upon registration (try the melody an octave higher), instrumentation, and composed adaptations.

Study of this song will show that, even in cases where a 3rds bass arrangement will probably prove successful at the outset, it is frequently worthwhile to explore the potential of the earlier processes too, as so often different processes are suitable for the same piece, for different purposes. **As always, no process (however 'simple') should ever be considered as 'outgrown'.**

(v)   The melody played with a two-note accompaniment makes an adequate setting of 'Down in Demerara'. Compose an improved version of this by altering the lower note of the pattern when it sounds in unison with a melody note. Compare your version with the Appendix, page 256.

2 Drink to Me Only

17th century English

Drink to me on-ly with thine eyes, And I will pledge with mine,
Or leave a kiss with-in the cup And I'll not ask for

wine. The thirst that from the soul doth rise Doth

ask a drink di-vine; But might I of Jove's

nec-tar sup, I would not change for thine.

Though less conspicuous to the eye, here is another scalic melody, so a 3rds bass harmony may prove suitable.

(i)   Test the first phrase with 3rds or 10ths.

(ii)   Add the constant thumb-note, repeating it beneath every melody note, until the cadence changes the process. Should you get stuck at bar 3, treat the first two quavers (which belong to a single syllable and only momentarily break the scalic line) as a unit, by dropping the bass an octave under the second quaver. The rest will then be obvious.

(iii)   Consider pace and texture. Is this primarily a drinking song, or primarily a love song? In the light of your decision, are you fully satisfied with the fullness of harmony?

In contrast to 'Down in Demerara' and the "hor-se-lum", this song is passionately emotional, rich in sentimental poetic imagery typical of its period. Though it needs to flow, at what might be called a caressing pace, it also needs to be slow enough for every quaver to possess some weight—unlike the typical ♩ ♪ rhythm most often associated with $\frac{6}{8}$. Above all it needs to be rich-sounding, rich with emotion and a really good wine. The mere inclusion of a single note within the outer 10ths provided suitable textures for 'This Old Man' and 'Down in Demerara', both fast, light songs. But this song requires more weight, more 'musical velvet'. It is not satisfied by a thin texture and requires fuller statement of the chords. This will require three notes at a time in the right-hand part.

177

(iv)   To add an extra note to the first chord, already complete, you will obviously double the E flat root of the chord, playing $e^{b\prime}$. Proceed, with both hands, adding an extra note of your choice between each melody note and repeated $b^{\flat}$ thumb-note. Then listen carefully to the result and see if any small improvements are necessary.

In 'This Old Man' the tiny phrase "give a dog a bone" introduced the pattern:

Ex. 75

In 'Down in Demerara' this device became essential at a more important pace, the outset of the song:

Ex. 76

In 'Drink to Me Only' it becomes necessary to master the manual habit of doubling back from keynote to leading note *within* the right-hand part. It is most important to retain the thumb-note (5th degree) as this serves as an anchor, without which the hand is liable to lose its whereabouts. These notes only have subsidiary musical importance and will not normally be in the forefront of your mind as you work. It is a matter of developing the craft of slipping your 2nd finger down and back again inside the chord, like this:

Ex. 77a

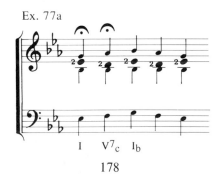

I   V⁷c   Ib

A common mistake is to begin:

$$\text{V}^7{}_c \quad \text{I}_b$$

This gives $\text{V}^7{}_c$ two 5ths and no 3rd and involves parallel octaves with the bass. Such haphazard filling in may then produce doubled 3rds on the I_b where the 3rd is already present in the bass. In avoiding the doubled 3rd of $\text{V}^7{}_b$ in bar 2, there is only room for *two* right-hand notes and a second *d'* in the right hand must be avoided. (In writing this for a four-part choir, altos and tenors will both sing the *b♭*.) 'Drink to Me Only' is ideal for learning to fill in these middle notes correctly, as it is slow and involves much repetition. But when you have mastered the sequence, see that you play it rhythmically.

The sequence of the first three beats ($\text{I-V}^7{}_c\text{-I}_b$) involves what is known as the *passing 2nd inversion*. In contrast to the arresting effect of the cadential 2nd inversion, which acts like a brake drawing a phrase to a halt, the passing 2nd inversion is very smooth in effect, with the phrase well under way. The chord needs no special attention and arises naturally out of the horizontal process, a single process bringing in train many additional chords and inversions, for but a single thought!

(v)   As the first phrase constitutes three-quarters of the song, being repeated and finally recapitulated, there remains only the intervening phrase. A 3rds bass beneath these bars, which consist of the chord of E flat, would produce the chord of C minor, and complete confusion of tonality. So this is a place to revert to the simplest support for the key chord, perhaps an arpeggio (as on page 143) at the beginning of each bar, until a return to the 3rds bass becomes appropriate. When it does, use the thumb-note that fits the melodic *c"* and the following notes. So the texture will remain thinner in this section, and this will lead naturally into the correct right-hand interval for the imperfect cadence bar. How many bass notes are needed in that bar to satisfy the phrasing? If in doubt, say the words.

Finally let passion rule, and double the bass in octaves for the recapitulation. It is only possible to do this if your *right* hand is playing the thumb-note: the *bass* in harmony needs a *full half* of your attention.

(vi)   Play the whole song in E, instead of E flat. Once you have mastered the hand patterns in one key, the other will not prove difficult.

3 Begone, Dull Care!

17th century English

Be - gone, dull care! ___ I pri-thee be gone from me! ___ Begone, dull care! ___ You and I shall nev-er a - gree. ___ My
wife shall dance and I will sing, So mer-ri-ly pass the day, ___ But i'
faith, dull care, ___ Thou nev-er shall have thy way. ___

(i)   Make your own arrangement before you read on, so that you can compare your unaided setting.

(ii)   There is a Jacobs fairy story about a mother who sent her son, Lazy Jack, to the market. When he returned she told him how he should have transported his purchases home. His capacity for obedience surpassing his ability to reason intelligently for himself, on each next marketing day he brings what he has bought according to the latest instructions. Having first carried home a cat, he returns next time with the joint of meat on a lead, and so forth! Techniques, the tools of the trade, can be taught; but good judgement is a matter of personal choices in the light of each new context. The more you learn, the wider the field of choice and the more important it becomes to exercise good judgement in respect of every aspect of a piece; form and phrasing, tempo, dynamic and touch qualities, together with subject matter and words in the case of a song or descriptive piece. All those aspects need to be considered here.

Compare these variants with each other and with your own setting, then make your own judgement as to which are most suitable. Combine the treble of one with bass of another if you wish.

Although the discrepancies may seem slight, the majority of people tend to select the variants for which there seem to be some basic aesthetic justification. It is usually easier to recognise a setting that seems 'just right' than to produce one, so you may set criteria of general value from investigating your critical reactions to these versions.

Pay attention to the words of the song: the most important thing to bring out in the piece is the alternation between stark and flowing passages, using different processes for each.

Ex. 78

Bars 1 and 2

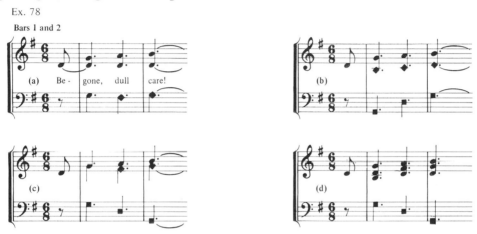

How far do you agree with these assessments?

- **(a)** is too weak for the words.
- **(b)** the 6ths are too smooth and lyrical, almost 'slushy': this is due to the c' of the Dominant 7th in the middle chord.
- **(c)** is preferable, for it suggests a clean, simple Dominant chord, without a 7th; but it is too thin.
- **(d)** the right hand combined with the left hand of (c), with its contrary-motion bass, seems stronger.

- **(e)** may seem farcical, but is in fact the style of setting for another version of the melody, to very different words, as the opening of a sentimental French cabaret song. There the tempo is much slower, the texture smoother, and though the landscaping I-V-I is common to both songs, in this case the inclusion of the 7th of the Dominant chord is stylistically right, and the weaker bass line suitably unobtrusive. In a different key it becomes even more suitable:

Ex. 79

Andante

The initial chords, I-V-I, are now thought of vertically and the former easy hand-pattern of continuous 6ths has been replaced by the three different right-hand patterns:

Ex. 80

The texture of unbroken right-hand 6ths to which you are accustomed greatly facilitates the beginnings of keyboard harmony and extemporisation, building up confidence and skill. But at the present stage the modifications and additions involved in playing the fuller chords above should present no problems. (If you knew someone as a child you will generally recognise the grown-up.) From now on, you must discriminate between the effect of Dominant 7th and that of plain Dominant, listening critically and using good judgement as to which is preferable in each context. There is nothing sillier than the blanket rejection of the Dominant 7th, as though it were out of fashion. It is simply appropriate in some contexts and out of place in others.

The remaining extracts in Example 78 produce questions

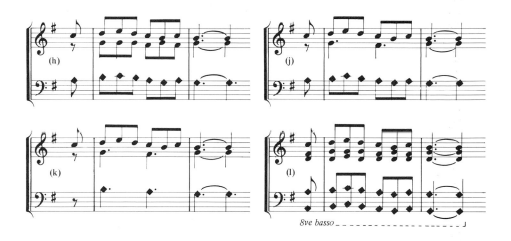

(**f**) to (**r**)   The potential of 3rds bass is like that of a plant which may grow from a sapling to a substantial bush but may then need pruning, according to its situation. If you want a thick solid hedge, keep as many small branches as possible: if you want a graceful slender growth, cut the texture down to a mere profile: if you want a noble forest tree, allow it to expand and add further weight. From these variants, locate the equivalents of the sapling, the hedge, the slender tree and the noble specimen. Which variants do you find best suited to the present song? Though the simple 3rds of (f) and (g) may be dismissed as mere germinating seedlings, it is worth noting that even these might be eligible for an ultimate arrangement. For though it might seem to provide an excessive contrast to the first phrase in a piano arrangement, and (j) or (k) be preferred, orchestration tolerates and often needs greater contrasts. Handel, in 'The Arrival of the Queen of Sheba' (*Solomon*) writes this passage for two oboes:

Ex. 81

in direct contrast to 'full' sections for string orchestra, spanning a five octave register.

Does anything worry you when you *look* at example (k)?

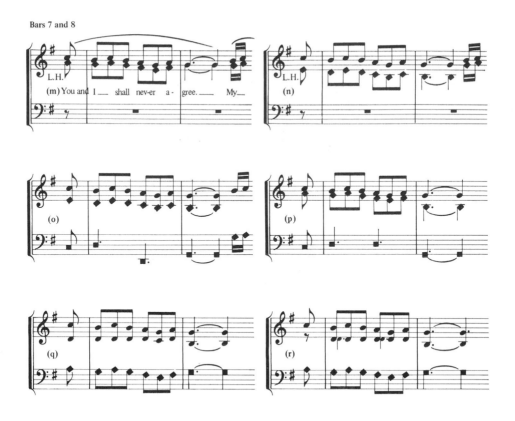

Does anything worry you when you *play* example (q)? If so, is (r) preferable?

Can you discover why similar adaptation is not necessary in examples (j) and (k)?

You should now be able to manage 'doubling back' between keynote and leading note with the right-hand thumb, when it is preferable for the texture to exclude the constant anchoring fifth degree. What might influence your choice between (o) and (p), with bass considered interchangeable? The passage can obviously be treated effectively by either 3rds or 6ths. Thirds carry the potential of 3rds bass, as in (r), but, as has been found in earlier examples, 6ths over a sparse solo bass makes a stronger main cadence. The bass at (p) might be preferable in the middle of the song, the extra strength of the 'HXB' cadence being reserved for the final cadence.

Combing through for 5ths

The error behind the 'sin' of parallel 5ths is not the consecutives themselves (see (q)) but in the use of adjacent chords in similar motion with the melody. Neighbouring 5ths (even when in inside parts) tend to evoke adjacent chords, because 5ths have the power to generate their own harmonic series . . . *as long as the 5ths are 'perfect'*. In (h), (j) and (k), although the 5ths *look* the same as those in (q), they sound different: one of each pair is a diminished 5th and cannot generate the sound of adjacent chords. See the harmonic series, *e'-b♭'* on page vi. So there is no need to worry about (h), (j) or (k) as long as you *hear* the diminished 5ths: combing through for 5ths by eye is useless.

Bars 10 to 13

Examples (s) and (t) sound equally well and either may be used, perhaps in different verses; or (s) might change to 3rds bass when the running quavers recur in bar 11. If you have any doubts as to which version is preferable for bar 12, sing the words. The origin of the cadential $^6_4$ (I$_c$) in (t) was shown in the Appendix, page 244. Yet it is surprising how long it takes some students to *feel* the need for only one bass note in such cases—which must, of course, fit the final melodic note. Otherwise the slurred phrasing is destroyed and nonsense made of a single-syllabled word. The middle section of 'Drink to me only' (page 177) ended similarly. To master this cliché once and for all, play this in various registers, in rapid succession and in various keys:

Ex. 82

4 Theme and Variations (Mozart)

Andante Grazioso

Opening of Piano Sonata in A, K.331

See how many of the processes learnt so far appear in this composition, by analysing its structure and memorising its 'patterns'.

(i)   Play the Theme throughout. Repeat it, playing repeated e's as thumb-notes in the right hand instead of the left. Then see how easily and quickly you can memorise the first three bars. Notice how Mozart avoids parallel 5ths between chords IV and V in bar 3 by retaining the 5th degree as thumb-note (as you did in (r) of example 78).

(ii)   Noting that the phrase ending is the cadential I_c-V you have just been practising, complete the phrase from memory.

(iii)   Noting that the cadence in bar 8 is 'fuller', over 'HXB' bass, play the first *eight* bars from memory.

(iv)   Analyse the melodic and chordal structure created by left and right-hand arpeggios in bars 9 to 12 and note the phrased I_c-V cadence again. Play bars 1 to 12 from memory, In bar 12, if you compare the sound of $d^{\natural\prime}$ with the written $d^{\sharp\prime}$ you will never forget the right note.

(v)   In the recapitulation from bar 13 onwards, Mozart does not repeat bars 1–8 exactly but contracts them to one set of four bars followed by a two-bar 'tailpiece' (coda). Compare the cadence in bar 16 with that most like it in the first eight bars. Analyse the structure of the coda noting

186

the need to play inner *c*'s with right thumb. Play the whole theme from memory.

You will realise from this piece of musical analysis that the methods you are using are those which, to composers of Mozart's day, became a 'language' everyone understood. By bringing your aural and analytical powers to help your fingers, you can more easily remember the sound of that language. Developing a Mozartian clarity of harmonisation must be an advantage; for a limpid texture can always be thickened, clouded or even contradicted later . . . intentionally. It is much harder to learn how to 'thin out' an unwieldy texture.

(vi)   The Variations which follow can be played, analysed and perhaps memorised, using the same procedures, by those with sufficient technique to play them. But pianists *and* non-pianists can investigate the score by eye to locate processes which have been studied.

It may help in Variations I and II to play the bass notes on the beat *only* together with the right-hand part to appreciate the 3rds bass construction. If you find Variation III difficult, landscape it with primary 5ths first.

In Variation V, notice how soon after commencing with the 'Alberti' bass Mozart modifies it, in fact combining it with a 3rds bass (see page 176). In which variation does the theme sound faster, No. V or No. IV?

16 COMBINING THE PROCESSES

A complete list of shorthand signs is now available to you:

Sign	Description
8	Octaves
T5	Tonic 5th 'drones'
I/V	5ths of I and V only
Pr5	Primary 5ths
$\overline{5}$	Solo melody over various 5ths
3/6	3rds and 6ths only
3/6̲	3rds and 6ths over single-line bass
$\frac{3/6̲}{5}$	3rds and 6ths over primary 5ths
6th Acc.	Independent accompaniment of bass note followed by upper 6th
$\overline{3}$	3rds bass

The extent to which these single concepts carry the player over whole areas of music, in contrast to the unproductive vertical construction of constituent chords, will be shown further in these next songs.

1 Leave her, Johnny

English Sea Shanty

I thought I heard the skip-per say, *Leave her, John - ny, leave her!* 'To-mor-row you will get your pay:' *It's time for us to leave her.*

188

(i) Using the shorthand signs, write a working process for the four phrases and compare with the Appendix, page 256 44(a).

(ii) Write out the melody. Label the chords vertically produced by the working process and compare with the Appendix, page 256 44(b).

(iii) Memorise the melody. Write down by name the cadence you prefer at the end of each phrase, under the melody.

(iv) Play the song, using the working process of the Appendix, page 256 44(a) and analyse the cadences as you hear them. Compare the cadences you play with your *written* preference in (iii) above. Are they the same? If not, which do you consider most suitable and why?

Considerations of form should guide the decision on whether $\frac{}{3}$ should lead to chord VI in the cadence at bar 6 or not: in this case, a 3rd below the tonic is not necessarily out of place and proves an asset.

(v) Compare your final setting with the Appendix, page 256 44(c), and read on.

2 Donkey Riding
If you cannot remember the tune, refer to page 122.

Treat this song by each process separately:

(i) $\frac{}{5}$

(ii)   3/6

(iii) $\frac{3/6}{5}$

(iv) $\frac{}{3}$ (Notice that there is no objection to a sustained *c′* thumb-note in bars 2 and 12.)

(v)   Make a final arrangement, mixing the processes as you wish.

3 The Bells of Aberdovey

Welsh

If to me as true thou art,— As I'm true to thee, sweet-heart,—

We'll hear, one, two, three, four, five, from the bells of A - ber - do - vey.

189

Decide straight away which final textures to use, according to the pace at which accents need to fall. In the first pair of bars the melodic line rather than the words governs this, and singing it will best reveal the answer. See the Appendix, page 257 for further comment.

4 Will ye no come back again
If you cannot remember the melody, refer to page 115.

(i)   See if you can replay the song straight off by $\frac{3/6}{5}$. If you find this difficult, re-do each process separately. In any case, treat bars 11 and 12 by both $\frac{3}{5}$ and $\frac{6}{5}$.

(ii)   In phrases where you use upper 3rds, change them to $\frac{\ }{3}$. If it is suitable to change mid-phrase, do. You will find that this mixture of processes produces a very satisfactory setting.

Further Songs

Treat these songs mostly by $\frac{\ }{3}$, using thin or thick texture according to the context.

One Man went to Mow (see page 44)

Captain Morgan's March (see page 22)

Which section is still best treated as you first set the melody? Which section can benefit from later processes? Which simply needs to have the original skeleton filled in? (See Appendix, page 257.)

Camptown Races (see page 23)

Compare the treatments you find suitable for "meadow" in 'One Man went to Mow' and "Doo-dah" in this song.

Oh, Susanna

Shenandoah

Although this is slow, keep the recitative-like flow by not repeating the thumb-note too frequently.

Gallery Carol

English, West Country

This song moves by the bar, not the written beat. The pulse will be established by slow thumb-notes: tie the anacrusis to the first one. What will be the best nearby bass note beneath the second note in bar 1? Keep the movement going under the dotted note by anticipating the pre-cadential bass note.

This Endris Night

The Holly and the Ivy (see page 71)

Keep the verse very light, mostly in two parts only. Keep the repeated *g*'s solo (or doubled in the chorus) and tie the last one as you go into 3rds bass.

Gloucestershire Wassail

English, West Country

Octave doubling will make a good start. You could add zip to the last line by a one-bar pace cadential bass, with drop of register to fill each second beat and rests under the anacrusic third beats.

17 PULLING OUT ALL THE STOPS

This chapter is concerned with what is generally regarded as full harmony, moving in block chords at a one-beat pace, a simple form of hymnal harmony. This is still largely achieved by horizontal concepts, mainly that of $\frac{-}{3}$. By this process such a large proportion of each piece is successfully harmonised that the errors (or gaps) can be dealt with in relation to the surrounding texture. It is never a matter of working chord-by-chord into a void.

In 'Begone, Dull Care', you have already considered some chords as vertical units, like individual pillars of sound. These pillars, for all their individual emphasis, tend to appear in short groups which, though the horizontal flow of a single *manual* interval disappears, can still be brought to mind as a single unit.

It should be easy to master the adaptations necessary to change, for example 'Lavender's Blue':

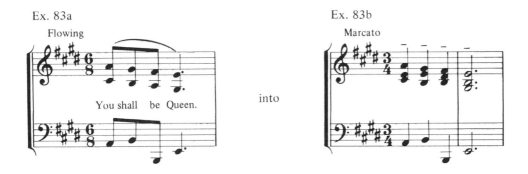

In only one of those chords has the 6th disappeared (and you have already practised shifting the 2nd finger between keynote and leading note in the $\frac{-}{3}$ work of Chapter 15). Once the right hand has mastered these shifts, the pattern will of course be the same in every key (except for the necessary variants of black and white notes). This sequence should now be thought of as the unit lower tetrachord of the key concerned, in this case *descending*. Reverse the right hand exactly for the *ascending* lower tetrachord. Try it over the same bass. The cadential I_c proves its role by acting as an irrelevant brake on the harmony as it begins to gain momentum. Root position is essential beneath the 3rd degree of the scale here:

Ex. 83c

I   V   I   IV

The 'HXB' unit is not relevant to the ascending version, where the bass will be thought of as establishing the root chords I-V-I-IV; but the four chords should still be conceived as a tetrachordal unit.

The same melodic line could also be treated by $\frac{}{3}$:

Ex. 83d

So long as the ear is satisfied, the different chord positions do not matter. In neither case think of *notes*: be guided by the degree of strength or flow needed for the passage concerned. The $\frac{}{3}$ treatment is weaker here than the version consisting of root positions... but the latter may be good for the first verse of a song and a $\frac{}{3}$ better for a later, gentler verse. Choice of right-hand 6ths, or chords shaped as in Example 83b, depends on whether a plain V or the more velvety V^7 is preferable in a context. When it seems out of place, as at the beginning of 'Begone, Dull Care', V^7 is apt to sound 'smudgy'; but in many contexts it is essential to the style. Critical listening is needed.

The other addition to your repertoire in the last chapter came from the discovery that, when using $\frac{}{3}$, it is no longer necessary to reject automatically a 3rd below the keynote. In a major key this *will* imply a minor harmony (chord VI), which can on occasion be very appropriate. It can also establish an Interrupted Cadence, so avoiding what might otherwise have been a premature Perfect Cadence. The form of a piece will be the guide as to when you allow a 3rds bass to lead to chord VI, and when not. So, though it may be reached by a horizontal process, the particular character of chord VI will be considered something of a singular event perceived vertically, even though it may be produced by a horizontal working process.

1 Unto Us a Boy is Born

Piae Cantiones 1582

Un - to us a boy is born! King of all cre - a - tion, Came he to a world for - lorn, The Lord of ev - 'ry na - - - - - - - tion.

This well-known carol has five verses. A selection from the processes that have been studied will enable you to play different arrangements for each verse, building up gradually to a climax in the last verse in the manner of an organist 'pulling out all the stops'. Some valuable new learning will be involved in the process.

First Three Verses

For the first three verses make a selection from the following processes. Play through all of them. First draw phrase marks on your copy; see that they tally with the lines of the verse.

(i)   T5 can be effective as a simple ground rhythm, perhaps for a nativity play, accompanying a group of peasants out-of-doors moving rather than singing, with the dancers' drum represented on the piano. Choose carefully which beats of the bar you use for the 'drum'.

(ii)   Pr5 would be better for singing. A single 5th will serve for each bar but one, where there will be a choice if you phrase the melody well.

(iii)   Try $\frac{6}{5}$ throughout. Now you will see that the phrasing at the end of bar 6 requires a rest under the last crotchet anacrusis.

(iv)   Try $\frac{}{3}$ throughout. You will find where 3rds bass can be used, though not necessarily suitably.

(v)   Try $\frac{3}{5}$ with minimum necessary 6ths. Notice where $\frac{3}{5}$ and $\frac{6}{5}$ involve alternative harmonies.

(vi)   Try a chosen selection of $\frac{3/6}{5}$.

(vii) Select three of the above processes to set the first three verses.

Hymnal Treatment of Verse 4

(i)   The strong, joyous marching quality of this verse calls for a lively crotchet tread, one chord for each note . . . "lead us all". You should be able to make a gratifying first attempt at this if you recognise each area of melody marked by a square bracket as a 'unit' for which you are able to provide a four-part treatment. Do the best you can with bar 5 in the meantime. Try now, in four parts:

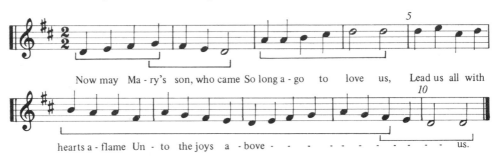

(ii)   Note any areas that you think could be improved.

(iii) Consider the following advice concerning areas which you may not have solved to your satisfaction:

   (a)   Though you will have recognised bars 3–4 as consisting of the ascending upper tetrachord of the scale, you may have been critical of the sounds produced by $\frac{}{3}$: on what grounds? If you do not hear it, 5ths at a crotchet pace will reveal the problem. To reveal a problem is not to solve it; so try the next process, treatment by 3/6. Your chosen combination of these intervals should provide you with a lower part which, when dropped in register (and strengthened in bar 4) will provide you with a good bass. Arrange this passage in *three* parts; so you only have to find a thumb-note. For how long does one thumb-note apply? When it needs changing, which note do you prefer—*a'* or *g'*—and where will that lead? You now have a new unit, with which to harmonise the *ascending upper tetrachord* of a scale, avoiding the pitfall of parallel IV-V, which root treatment of degrees 6–7 would involve, but which IV-V^{7}c avoids. (V^{7}c here does not have to have an *a'* in it: the cadence is still Perfect. Remember this for future use.)

196

(b)   Bar 5 was satisfactorily landscaped by Tonic 5th, the melody being interpreted as the keynote interspersed with passing notes above and below (like a 'turn' ornament). Can you see this bar another way? If you place a pencil point down the centre of the bar, what does this reveal? Which upper interval did you prefer in this bar, 3rd or 6ths? As the previous phrase ended with repeated *d"*s on chord I, which alternative chord containing the keynote will provide the best contrast here? Play its root, beneath right-hand 6th, then *drop* to another secondary chord root beneath the next 6th. Treat the rest of the bar sequentially. You will find that to bring your bass (which has twice dropped a 5th and risen a 4th) up a 4th again will bring you neatly into $\frac{}{3}$ for virtually the rest of the carol.

(c)   But you may find that rather monotonous. Notice the extended last phrase of the carol. Where would you have expected the melody to end, had the phrase lengths been symmetrical? At that point, how can you make the harmony justify the further extension, before finality is reached, so that these last bars do not sound like a record-player needle stuck in a groove.

(d)   You may even feel that the bass at this point would be strengthened by *not* following the melody up again (from bass B) in $\frac{}{3}$ but by continuing downwards, in contrary motion to the melody. If the crotchet-paced bass soon meets with a discord, simply run over that hurdle as a quaver passing note, when all will be well. Notice then that doubled major 3rds (F sharp in bass and melody) do *not* sound bad within a stepwise contrary motion passage, so continue the bass down to E, forming chord II in root position.

(e)   The most climactic ending can then be achieved by reversion to the landscaping chord for the whole penultimate bar, as a Dominant Pedal octave bass under melodic 6ths.

(f)   To keep the crotchet movement going to the final minim, insert under beats 2 and 3 of the last bar the kind of cadence which involves the keynote in both of its chords. (See Example 49, page 114).

(g)   While it is still in the grasp of your hands *and* mind *and* ears, repeat the whole verse in the key of C. Manual pattern and a little reasoning will see you through.

(h)   Translate the whole into the Tonic minor. Make your own decisions about which variants of the 6th and 7th degrees sound best. Notice again that working in terms of system

197

concepts, as opposed to being preoccupied with individual chords, will lead you to try things you might otherwise never have thought of.

Final Verse: Putting the Melody into the Bass

Now play verse 5 which could be made still more of a climax simply by playing the previous arrangement with the bass doubled in octaves. But beware of developing the habit of automatically doubling basses in octaves whether or not it is suitable to the context. There is a more interesting way of making this final verse into a climax. That is to put the melody itself into the bass line and add the harmony above. In a scalic melody such as this, it can easily be done, for the most part, if you treat that *bass* melody as the lower part of $\overline{3}$, adding the top part a 3rd (*i.e.* 10th) above, filling in between.

(a) It is vital to follow the bass melody aurally, while you are playing chords above it. So first of all play the melody solo, starting on *d* in the bass stave. When you come to add the texture above, always play the bass a little louder.

(b) In phrase 1, play a *three-note* right hand texture above, by treating the bass line as $\overline{3}$.

(c) In phrase 2, as in the previous verse, remember the simple treatment by close position 3rds or 6ths. Raise the bass to do this. What do you discover on comparing the result with the same treatment of that phrase when the melody was on top? Add thumb-note where there is room.

(d) In phrase 3, bar 5 will be solved on the same inversionary principle. Here the 'binding notes' in common between each pair of chords, crotchets which were previously inserted *within* the 6ths, are most effective tied as minims at the top of the three-part texture, flowing smoothly into bar 6.

(e) In phrase 4, after the first anacrusic note where the top part needs to drop to *d'*, the rest can be treated by $\overline{3}$, so long as the top part avoids a 3rd above the 5th degree of the scale. Why is this necessary? The top part naturally continues to flow until the final minim.

(f) If you drop the bass melody an octave, there will be room for a four-part texture, and you can even double the bass melody with the octave below.

Make your final selection for playing all five verses. Record the result and play it back, listening critically. If you really master this carol, with the variety of opportunities it offers, including putting the melody in the bass—and especially if you can do it in other keys—you have gone a long way towards achieving facility in keyboard harmony. What is more, what you are playing is clean and clear and well spaced.

Pulling Out All the Chords

Your full, rich harmonisation of 'Unto Us a Boy is Born' consisted almost entirely of primary chords, in root positions and inversions. Secondary chords were used on only four of the 36 harmonised beats in the verse 4 arrangement, . . . and less than four when the melody was in the bass. You used secondary chords VI and II at the beginning of bar 5:

(i)   Continue that sequence all the way down the scale, ending when this bar is repeated an octave below (a) in this example:

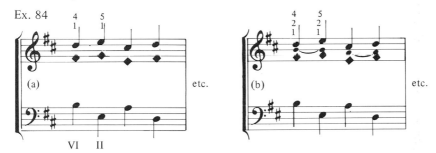

Repeat the sequence inserting the tied binding note as in (b) of the example, and then play it again, repeating that inner note on each crotchet.

(ii)   Play the sequence any of these ways, saying aloud the number of each chord used. This is easy as every bass note is the root of the chord.

(iii)   You may have hesitated each time you said 'chord VII', hearing a jarring sound, which is neither major nor minor but 'diminished'. The diminished interval was a 5th above the bass. Play the three notes of the triad—$c^{\#\prime}$-$e^\prime$-$g^\prime$—in close position with the right hand; then double each note in turn as a bass below the right-hand chord:

Which do you prefer and which do you like least?

199

All harmony of this kind builds in your ear from the bass, just as the harmonic series is founded on a 'bass' fundamental. If you now play each right-hand note *in turn* above the different basses you will hear that in the second chord, no individual right-hand note is discordant. In the first chord, $c^{\sharp\prime}$ above g is an augmented fourth—the 'Devil in Music', see page 238—and in the third, g' above $c^{\sharp\prime}$ is the diminished 5th you heard in the sequence above. In sequences such as this, much used by 18th-century composers, adherence to sequential pattern takes precedence over individual chord sound. When you listen to music of that period, see if you can recognise those passages.

This sequence uses the chords on every degree of the major scale for the first time. It shows how well chords combine whose roots are a 4th or 5th apart: and this is generally so whether they are root position or inversion. You will remember that chords with roots a 2nd apart need careful handling to avoid displeasing parallels (*e.g.* by inversion of one chord or by contrary motion between melody and bass) and that bass roots a 3rd apart *can* be effective but tend to sound modal rather than diatonic (*e.g.* I-III-V).

2 Good King Wenceslas

Piae Cantiones 1582

This is another carol requiring a one-beat harmonic pace, which you may be able to extemporise without any prior sketches, if you pay due consideration to the melodic structure. Recognise that the concepts 'right hand, left hand' mean a lot to the player, but nothing to the listener: so in bar 1 either repeat the full chord or the melodic g' only. Drop into $\frac{}{3}$ at the end of the first phrase. After you have completed your setting, answer the following questions:

(i) In bar 3, where did you need to depart from $\frac{}{3}$, and why?

(ii)   Is the final phrase symmetrical, followed by "Amen"?

(iii) If not, how should that impression be avoided?

(iv)   Where else did you use the same cadence?

18 SOME MODIFICATIONS

You should now be sufficiently accomplished in the use of $\frac{}{3}$, in textures of varying weight and speed, and prepared to switch to 6ths over cadential bass at the appropriate moments, to be ready to incorporate a couple of important modifications.

1 French Folk Song

French

(i)   This French folk tune is sometimes used as a hymn. A moderately fast and light one-beat pace, with a three-note texture throughout, will be suitable for either use. The prevalence of scalic passages suggests $\frac{}{3}$, with necessary divergences and modifications. Attempt this without prior landscaping. In several places there are alternative possible treatments by scalic bass. Select your choice, or make more than one arrangement.

(ii)   With what thumb-note did you start the first phrase? It is worth observing as a general principle that, for manual convenience, if a passage is *descending* it is best to start with a distant thumb-note. If a passage is *ascending*, choose a close one, so that the hand 'anchor' it provides allows sufficient rope for the extending melodic line. In this case, you will find an *f* too far away to anchor the whole phrase: use the *other* note common to all main beats and you will only need to double back under the quaver. The simpler consideration of hand comfort automatically leads to the same conclusion. Make a note of the harmonies produced on the first three beats by $\frac{}{3}$.

(iii)   Did you play the first three beats in bar 3 in sequence with those in bar 1? If not, do so now:

Ex. 86

Are you satisfied with this solution? It is perfectly possible, as the key has already been established. Or do you feel that the change from major harmonisation of the first bar to minor here is not really what the solo melody implies, and that there ought to be some solution which produces more similar 'rhyming' harmonisation of these two phrases? Try to find one.

(iv)   You should be able to call to mind another idea that would provide a good contrapuntal bass beneath. Include the appropriate thumb-note. Compare the harmonies of bar 1 with those you have now played in bar 3. (If necessary, page 154 will remind you of the bass required.)

(v)   In Chapter 12, this musical device was considered as counterpoint and was not analysed harmonically beyond the landscaping stage. All diatonic counterpoint carries *harmonic* implications. As a 6th is a 3rd inverted and a 10th is a 3rd wider separated, this two-part contrapuntal motif may be considered harmonically as a modification of $\frac{}{3}$. You will know from example 66 (page 156) that these two directions of melody combined at the same pitch (a) pass across a unison between the two 3rds. Interpreted as two scalic motifs across a 3rd and spaced wider apart (b), or in mirror pattern (c), that unison becomes an 8ve:

Ex. 87

If a right-hand thumb-note, sustained or repeated, is inserted between this counterpoint, harmonies are defined which were previously only implied. If the bass pattern is ascending across a 3rd indicating tonic harmony, you will be playing I-V_c-I_b, and when the bass is inverted mirrorwise to descend, you will be playing I_b-V_c-I. The chords are the same in both cases, only their positions vary. There is no more need for the player to think of the passage in terms of this theoretical analysis as three chords, than to think of the counterpoint as three intervals. The passage is simply a pattern made up of motif accompanied by its inversion. It most frequently involves Tonic Harmony sandwiching Dominant; but it can equally involve any other pair of chords with the same relationship, *i.e.* with roots a 4th/5th apart, as in the sequence derived from bar 5 of the carol, 'Unto Us a Boy is Born' (example 84a, page 199).

(vi) Familiarise yourself mentally and manually with this common musical progression by playing it in these various ways, first in the key of C then in B flat and any other key you wish. If the thumb-note is inserted, the *prevailing* chord will come to mind. Notice whether each unit is major or minor. Continue in sequence to the top of the scale in these different versions:

Ex. 88

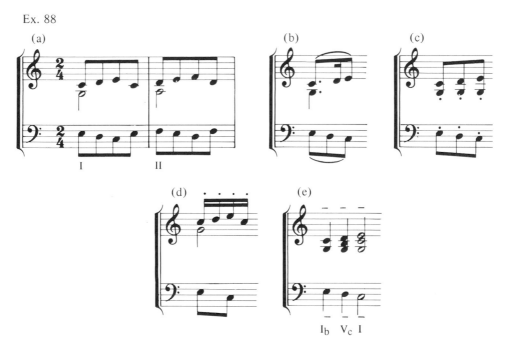

(vii) When this flowing counterpoint is filled out by a thumb-note or more, as at (e), the midway unison or octave becomes defined as the 2nd inversion of another chord. This again is a 'passing 2nd inversion' (see page 179). As you will hear, this has an opposite sound effect to that of a cadential 2nd inversion: it helps the music to flow, whereas the cadential $^6_4$ arrests it. The flow results from the scalic bass, which is why students are traditionally advised not to leap to a 2nd inversion in the middle of a phrase, as that will tend to sound as though it were a cadential arrest (unless it is within a bass line jumping from one inversion to another of the same chord). You will notice that as the outer parts change places across an octave, the doubling of the 5th in the 2nd inversion chord is inevitable.

(viii) This sequence makes it clear that the prime concept is pattern; for the melodic degrees and individual chords involved may vary. The second bar of (a) in example 88, involving an exchange between 2nd and 4th degrees of the scale, between root and 3rd of the chord II, is frequently very useful to precede a Perfect Cadence. Remember this. The general principle of $\frac{}{3}$ involves a bass line running parallel to the melody. The modification which, for obvious triadic reasons can only apply to a 3-step (or, occasionally, a 5-step) scalic motif, may be regarded as *inverted* or *contrary* 3rds *bass*. There is scope for both in this and the other songs in this chapter.

(ix) Decide what structural role the remainder of bar 3 to 4 fulfils, then play the first four bars of the song. In bars 5 and 6, try both parallel and contrary $\frac{}{3}$. Then find the appropriate thumb-note to establish the harmony each bass line implies. Both treatments are equally valid.

(x) A variety of sketches may be needed to lead you to a good solution in bars 7 and 8:

(a) Do 6ths sound satisfactory? (b) Do 3rds sound satisfactory?

(c) Plays 6ths again.

(d) This time *sing* a lower line of 3rds and only afterwards play what you sang:

Ex. 89a

It is instructive to note that the voice may instinctively solve what baffles the brain.

(e) Add any bass notes of which you feel certain, to the 6ths or 3rds.

(f) Put the lower line of 3rds (in which you no doubt discovered the need to modify the sixth crotchet) down in register to form $\frac{}{3}$ and find the appropriate thumb-notes. You will probably want to strengthen the bass at the end of the phrase, adapting middle notes to suit. You will now have established a clear 'modulation' to the Dominant key. This may have come to you easily, or it may not. Knowing what to *do* to produce sounds that your ear anticipates is not easy, as your hearing may often be in advance of your 'knowledge'. Simply floundering around from note to note in search of improvements may only lead to further confusion and frustration, for the sense of context becomes obscured. This is one reason why definite processes are helpful.

Most people's conception of keys derives from instrumental scale practice, leading to the tacit assumption that a change of key will be manifested by the presence of accidental sharps, flats or naturals. But many a melody *implies* an essential modulation without traversing the degree of the new scale needing an accidental. Even a harmonisation may not do so:

Ex. 89b

(g)   You may well have played this in bars 7 and 8, and found it perfectly satisfactory. The discovery you have just made in close 3rds on the penultimate beat is still relevant, though the root position cadence makes a better bass. You may equally well have chosen to treat the passage by contrary $\frac{-}{3}$:

Ex. 89c

What therefore is the obvious bass note to insert for that fourth beat? What degree of the *original scale* has been modified both in the previous descending parallel 3rds and in this contrary bass? What degree of the *new key* has this established?

(xi)   Now return to parallel $\frac{-}{3}$ and make a fuller texture—though this is too plodding for a folksong—with four-note chords, three notes in the right hand on every beat beginning:

Ex. 89d

Unless you play by ear instinctively, or are so accustomed to playing hymns that you are perhaps *only* able to extemporise in that style, it is unlikely that you could have played that version off the cuff. These various approaches have shown that a modulation tends to happen gradually, like the change from dark to daylight, though there must be no doubt when it has finally dawned. For the raising of the 4th degree of the original key to become the 7th degree of the new key (its leading note) has occurred in three different places (and been implied in one) in the last four approaches. To fix these in your vocabulary, follow the Appendix, page 257.

In every case you will have raised the E flat by horizontal listening, within the surrounding context, not by considering the vertical construction of any chord in isolation.

(xii) The rest of the piece is recapitulation. Play the whole, in whichever detailed arrangement you choose.

2 The Harmonic Series

The harmonic series has been shown to be a sequence of sounds which may coincide vertically or evolve horizontally, so forming the basis of a musical texture in which faster-moving sounds from the upper areas progress over slower-moving lower sounds, stated or implied. A melody harmonised by $\frac{}{3}$ is seen to derive from a combination of the 3rd and 4th octaves of the series (see example 73, page 172). The scale in the 4th octave ($c''-c'''$) contains the vocabulary of *two major scales*: F, with 4th degree $b^{\flat}'''$, and C (its dominant key) with 7th degree $b^{\natural}'''$. Modulation from tonic to dominant key is therefore a natural evolution within the harmonic series, the minor chord on the 2nd degree of any tonic key (here $g'-b^{\flat}'-d''$) easily becoming a major chord ($g'-d''-b^{\natural}''$, whose fundamental, g, was 5th of the *original* series), chord V of the dominant key. This different placing of g' minor and g' major chords in the series probably explains why minor 3rds can be close-placed and doubled more satisfactorily than major 3rds, which need to be more widely spaced.

3 A-Roving

This is an easy song in which to put into practice what you have just been learning. Some further tips are:

(i)   To make the first two bars blend with the rest, first use $\frac{6}{5}$ as in example 90a, then break up the 5ths beneath into quavers as in example 90b:

Ex. 90

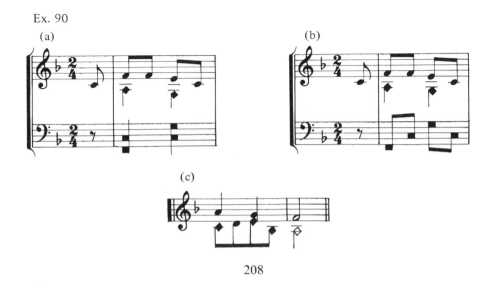

208

(ii)   In bars 5, 6 and 7 use one thumb-note per bar.

(iii)   In example 74b (page 174), quaver pace was maintained beneath melodic crotchets by playing the 6ths *after* the melody notes. That would sound rather weak in the richer harmonic texture of this song. Particularly at cadences, the related pattern of example 90c is useful.

4 A Virgin Unspotted

(i)   Add phrase marks to your copy, mostly but not all two-bar. Appreciation of anacrusic phrasing has been encouraged by the land-scaping process, which leaves anacruses solo. But remember, from the second phrase of 'Begone Dull Care' (example 78, page 183) that $\frac{}{3}$ can 'pair' a melodic anacrusis and the entry of the thumb-note will provide the main beat accent.

209

(ii)   As this is a flowing melody, keep the crotchet movement going under the dotted notes by a bass note on the second beat. Avoid making the recurrent cadence sound emphatically final every time: find a way of lightening it on earlier occasions.

(iii)   Play bass $b^{\flat}$ under the anacrusis at the end of bar 8. Whether or not you add a c' thumb-note, the harmony is the third (last) inversion of the Dominant 7th chord (V^7_d), a lovely and very useful chord. You have used it, in 'Sur le Pont d'Avignon' and many of the songs landscaped on I and V only in Part II, as the two-note accompaniment figure:

Ex. 91

This progression is particularly useful when two melodic beats require Dominant and Tonic harmonisation, but *not* the strength of root positions—passages with a buoyant feeling of flow, whether mid-stream or in a light 'take-off' like this. What pattern does this lead to in bar 9? Hold your bass note at the beginning of bar 10, with its thumb-note, for two beats and play the melodic d'' solo.

5 Robin Adair

210

If you diagnose the melodic structure intelligently, you will only need two of the processes studied in this and the preceding chapter to extemporise a three-part, one-beat pace, harmonisation of most of this song. But the central section is quite difficult to treat in the same style, so landscape it first.

(i)   Think of your landscaping chord in bar 10 as a new key, the Subdominant of A. For modulation, it is useful to visualise a Dominant key as up a 5th, a Subdominant key as down a 5th. Therefore the procedure for modulating (a) from Tonic 'up' to Dominant simply needs to be reversed to modulate (b) from Tonic 'down' to Subdominant. So where in (a) you would *raise* the 4th degree to become 7th of a Dominant key, in (b) you need to *lower* the 7th degree to become 4th of the Subdominant key. (Confirm this by observing in example 73, page 172, what raising b' to b'', or lowering $b^{\natural}''$ to $b^{\flat}'$, can signify in terms of key relationships.) You have lately linked the first 'tone' in the series, $b^{\flat}$-c', with chord $V^7{}_d$. The *equivalent* keynote and flattened leading note will give you $V^7{}_d$ of the key you need for bars 9–10 here.

Ex. 92

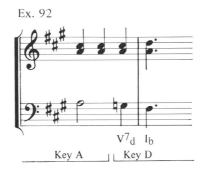

$V^7{}_d$ I_b

Key A   Key D

This will only be a 'passing' modulation as there is no opportunity to establish the key of D on the rest of the phrase, but it is a very attractive use of $V^7{}_d$ with which to expand your vocabulary. Carry the bass on down to *d*.

(ii)   In bars 11–12, what will make a good bass for the first 4 crotchets and what cadence will this lead to?

Modulations to the Dominant key are essential in a vast number of pieces. But modulations to the Sub-dominant are quite rare. **Remember that Primary keys, as chords, should not be thought of in arithmetical order, but as I, V and IV.**

6 Silent Worship

Opening of Aria from 'Ptolemy'

1 Did you not hear my la - dy {
2 Sure - ly you heard my la - dy {
Go down the___ gar - den sing - ing?

Black -bird and thrush were sil - ent   To   hear   the___ al - leys ring - ing.   O
Si - lenc -ing all the song-birds   And   set - ting the al - leys ring - ing.   But

saw you___ not my la - dy {
sure - ly you see my la - dy {
Out   in   the___ gar - den___ there?

Sham - ing the rose and li - ly   For   she   is ___   twice   as fair.
Rival - ling the glit - tering sun-shine With a glo - ry of gold - en hair.

You should now be able to make an arrangement in Handelian style of the opening section of this lovely aria (to be completed in the next chapter). The words will indicate the pace of the song. Vary $\overline{}_3$ with contrary $\overline{}_3$, and make use of a light V^7_d-I_b (as bass degrees 4-3 under melodic degrees 7-8). There is also scope for passing modulation to the Dominant. What cadence will you choose in bar 6? After you have made your arrangement, try to obtain a printed copy for comparison. Any such copy will be someone else's arrangement as Handel wrote only the melody and the bass; so your own may be equally valid.

Further Carols

On Christmas Night (see page 70)

Lower the register of the bass on repeat of the first phrase.

Jesus, good above all other

Line 4 may suitably commence with chord II, if the preceding chord was well chosen. Did you find the modulation?

19 SHORT AND LONG

1 All Through the Night

Welsh

(i)   Play the melody. If the version you know has a different rhythm in bars 9 to 12, play it your way. Memorise it.

(ii)   Landscape bars 1 to 4. If you feel dissatisfied with a single chord in bar 2, cover the last beat crotchets of bars 1 and 2 with two pencils. What you see will dictate procedure for bar 2.

(iii)   How you arrange these chords will be dictated by style and pace. The Welsh have been famous for the rich harmonies of their choral singing for centuries. The song needs a full harmonisation with flow which necessitates harmonic movement under the dotted notes. In the previous chapter use of the 3-note motif led to the process of alternating the root and 3rd of a chord in the bass. That provides the ideal solution here. Play bars 1 and 2, then reverse the order of roots and first inversions, and choose which you prefer. Listen to your landscaped sketch and decide whether the first 5th in bar 2 suggests to you a minor or major harmony. Apply the inversionary pattern again. Does the choice of major or minor chord here influence which way up you play the bass pattern in bar 1: *G-B-c* or *B-G-c*?

The natural Primary landscaping I IV|V−−| proved inadequate because the sequential melodic structure of these two bars was visually obscured by the falling 3rd at the end of the first bar and rising 3rd at the end of the second bar—until you covered up those final beats. The

213

sequence then demanded that I-IV be matched by II-V. Such a situation demonstrates again the value of landscaping in 5ths because, if unspecified by the melody, it leaves the 3rd of the chord undefined and open to subsequent choice. In such a case as this both choices are valid.

The minor chord II is natural to the key: and the difference of interval

between 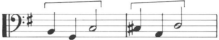 and is natural to the

scale of that key. But counting the semitones will show that the two sequences are not identical. This is called *tonal sequence*. If the C is made sharp, the interval patterns in the bass are identical and bar 2 becomes a *real sequence*:

This involves chromatic alteration of the tonic scale and the normal character of the chord or chords concerned. To what extent real sequence may establish a modulation or only convey the impression of a colourful 'chromatic' flux will depend upon the length of the passage concerned in relation to the piece as a whole . . . a matter of proportion.

(iv)   Harmonise bars 9 to 12. Melodic line, style and pace all indicate $\frac{}{3}$ as likely to prove effective in this central section. But you will be wise to try the passage in 10ths alone before deciding the thumb-note and subsequent further filling in. Where will you need to break away from $\frac{}{3}$? What clues have you concerning treatment at that point? An extra passing note should link the two processes. Be sure to phrase bar 12 well. If you are satisfied, add the recapitulation.

(v)   As your vocabulary enlarges, it becomes increasingly important to realise that there may be more than one valid setting of a passage, and to learn to discriminate between valid alternatives and errors. Practice in defending what you consider valid and explaining *why* you think something is 'wrong' develops judgement and self-confidence and prepares you to guide others. Can you find alternative applicable thumb-notes for a parallel $\frac{}{3}$ setting of bars 9-12? Then consult the Appendix, page 257.

(vi)   The second half of bar 10 is the same as the first half of bar 9. Using the thumb-note which establishes a prevailing minor harmonisation in these bars, are you satisfied by a return to the same bass note beneath that last crotchet of bar 10? What tonality seems to have been established in these two bars, in relation to the original key?

(vii)   If you raised the last $\frac{}{3}$ bass note in bar 10 by a semitone, how will you inflect it on the second beat of bar 11?

(viii) Though the *e'* thumb-note could be maintained throughout bar 11 there is a better possibility: listen to this bar in 10ths alone and see if you can find a more interesting solution for that third beat thumb-note. Once again, singing may help where eye or reasoning fail. Sing the 'thumb-note' line, while you play top and bottom:

Ex. 94

(ix)   The rhythm provides a clue to the process for bar 12, hinting at the recapitulation. Try to hear the dotted crotchet as an appoggiatura a 9th above the root of the chord II, recalling the treatment of bar 2. Whether you prefer chord II in its minor or major version, start with it as II$_b$ and it will lead naturally to the imperfect cadence of I$_c$-V. As last refinements, add a quaver passing note in the bass at the end of bar 11 restoring *d♯'* and a similar *c♮'* at the end of bar 12 to lead into the recapitulation.

(x)   Having discovered these modulations in a naturally evolving horizontal manner, you can now detach them from the flowing texture, where they were glove-fitted to the melody, and restructure them in terms of vertically conceived chords, to make an independent accompaniment under the vocal line of the song. This amounts to the chordal filling in of a new landscaping, which you can first do in 5ths. Remember that the passing modulations may have led you into A minor, E minor and D major and play a harp-style accompaniment for bars 9–12 consisting of V and I in each of the three keys, beginning:

Ex. 95

215

Remember also that a bass c^5 helped you to return to bar 13 in (ix) above...and remember the story of Lazy Jack who followed all his instructions to the letter. Having discovered it, do not turn every imperfect cadence into a chromatic creep up to the Dominant. From the beginning of this book, the importance of harmonic structure *in relation to form* has been emphasised; and form must indicate where you use a plain imperfect cadence and where to modulate to the Dominant. Beware of developing a habit of adding chromaticisms just for the hell of it. If inconsistently used they can lead to gimmicky or vulgar arrangements, perversions of the naturally implied harmonies of many a good melody, especially folk songs. But a *consistently* 'spiced' variation, which twists or departs from the obvious with a sophisticated sense of purpose is another matter. The artist should seek not only skill but, above all, good judgement, without which he may produce but 'sound and fury, signifying nothing'.

2 Piano Sonata Op. 49, No. 2 in G (Beethoven)

216

(i)   This extract shows the decorated cadence which ends the Exposition in the dominant key of D. Then the Development section of 14 bars begins with the chord of D minor (not the *key* of D minor). Play the extract: then identify the keys through which the section passes.

(ii)   Though shorter, the Exposition and Development of 'All Through the Night' are at least as well proportioned as this sonata movement. If you begin to sing the folksong's 'Development' section (bars 9 to 12) at bar 2 of Beethoven's Development section, you can hear the sonata as an accompaniment to the song (example 96a).

Ex. 96a

Continue bars 110 onwards (when the folksong no longer 'fits') and where the scale runs down into the Recapitulation, play *as* Recapitulation bar 13 of the song instead:

Ex. 96b

(iii)   Now observe and hear:

  (a)   the bass beneath the first dotted note in bar 121.
  (b)   the importance of leading notes ($g^\sharp$ in A minor, $d^\sharp$ in E minor).
  (c)   the use of the dominant note (5th degree) as off-beat pivot note in bars 106 to 110 (of A minor, then E minor) which becomes even stronger through bars 111 to 115 when e' itself becomes the dominant of A minor (bar 116) and a in turn becomes the dominant of D major (bar 117); d itself then

stays still in bar 118 and adds the flattened 7th of its *own* key, to become the chord V^7 of the original tonic (G) at the recapitulation of the opening theme.

(d) the $\overline{3}$ harmonisation of bar 107, plus left-hand off-beat thumb-note. (See 'Down in Demerara', page 174.)

3 Silent Worship

Second part of Aria from 'Ptolemy'

This is the central section of Handel's aria which you began in Chapter 18.

(i) Treat by $\overline{3}$, as you wish.

(ii)

(a) Landscape bar 9 on two primary 5ths of the tonic key (G).

(b) Exchange these for two alternative 5ths.

(c) Regard those two secondary chords as primaries of a related key. Returning to $\overline{3}$, what will you do to your first bass note? Match your thumb-note to the new harmony.

(d) You have a rest at the end of bar 9: make use of it to return to the tonic key in the bass and continue $\overline{3}$.

(e) What chord—now to be considered as a key—does $\overline{3}$ indicate for bar 11? Where will you first introduce the leading note of that key, and in which of the lower parts?

(f) What was the chord at the beginning of bar 11, in terms of key G? What is the role of that chord in bar 12, in terms of the key at the end of that bar?

(iii) You will now be able to play the whole aria (see page 212 for the first section). The piece is in ternary form (occasionally still called 'aria form'). In ternary form, contrast in the middle 'episode' is sometimes achieved by new thematic material and sometimes, as here, by development of the main material, involving a modulation at the end, and possibly subsidiary passing modulations. You will notice the similarity between your treatment of 'All Through the Night' and of this song which, though also 12 bars and recapitulation, contains more melody notes to a bar...and seems 'long' in proportion.

20 SEPARATE ACCOMPANIMENTS

1 Baa, Baa, Black Sheep (Quand Trois Poules)

There are many different versions of this song, in many countries and with different words, but this is the basic skeleton of the tune:

(i)   Copy the melody and, without playing it, write beneath each square bracket the treatment you would use for each section.

(ii)   Play the melody, adding solo bass line. Should you be dissatisfied, landscape in 5ths. (See the Appendix, page 258.)

(iii)   Fill in the implied harmonies at minim pace, repeating melodic crotchets only.

(iv)   The piece is an obvious candidate for an 'oom-pah' accompaniment. Play it, putting the melody up an octave and restructure the same harmonies in terms of low bass note followed by completion of each harmony with a three-part chord well above the bass note. Which position of the upper part of the chord sounds best?

Ex. 97a

Make a permanent mental and manual note of this. The *harmony* is of course in root position in every case, as that is always defined by the lowest bass note. When playing a bass note which represents a first inversion, omit the 3rd in the off-beat chord: double its 5th or its root instead.

(v) Ask someone else to play the melody in a high register, doubled at the octave (using both hands), while you play the previous accompaniment, with solo or octave bass and the upper chords with the right hand as before or enlarged. For example, though the 3rd should be omitted in example 97b, there is no objection to doubling the 3rds at 97c as both of them are in the right hand and high above the bass, where the 3rd is found in both the third and fourth octaves of the harmonic series. The further you progress the more apparent it will become that what sounds good or bad—or as you want it to, whatever that may be—is not just a matter of *what* notes, but of *where* they are:

(vi) It is salutary in this instance to try harmonising each 5th degree of the melody with chord V, as an example of how, even in so simple a context, use of a chord merely *calculated* to be applicable can prove disastrous. As early as Chapter 3, the restricted vocabulary of chords I and V^7 provided practice in this choice: and however advanced the work, care and aural imagination will continue to be needed for selection between these two Primary chords.

2 Harmonising the Major Scale

To accompany a descending major scale with a four-note chord to each degree (three notes in the right hand and one in the left) treat the task on the principal of 'counting songs' that add an extra item in each successive verse. Most of these revise ground already covered (as you learned to precede a Perfect Cadence by an increasing number of chords leading towards it, first by $\underline{6}$, then by fuller chords, not all following the same hand pattern). Listen carefully to make sure each chord makes a good progression with those on either side.

(i) Harmonise the following degrees in the key of C:

2-1

3-2-1

4-3-2-1

5-4-3-2-1

6-5-4-3-2-1

(ii) Check your result with the three bars in 'Baa, Baa, Black Sheep' where those degrees occur in scale order. Notice the importance of your choice to harmonise the 5th degree, so as to dovetail well with the chords on either side.

(iii)   Harmonise **8-7-6-5-4-3-2-1**. If you start from the top of the scale with a four-part Tonic chord, only the 7th degree remains to be allotted a chord. You will have been warned by (i) above against V preceding IV on a downward journey. What other chord contains the 7th degree?

At last a use is found for chord III in a major key, which can be beautiful in the occasional appropriate place, but simply wrong or tonally disruptive when over-used. Though III and IV are neighbouring chords, in harmonising the 6th and 7th degrees of a descending scale their roots move in contrary motion to the melodic line, so there is no problem of 'parallels'.

(iv)   Play ascending and descending versions in all keys, arranging the textures as you wish.

3 Harmonising the Minor Scale

Ascending minor scales may be treated in the same way as major, but descending minor scales—melodic or harmonic—must begin in contrary motion.

(i)   Start from a unison and play the melodic minor scale of C minor in two parts only, in contrary motion outwards.

(ii)   Repeat, filling in the implied harmonies as space allows as treble and bass separate.

(iii)   Do the same with the harmonic minor in contrary motion. Close treatment having clarified the harmonies, each scale can then commence an octave apart, leaving room for more enrichment between.

(iv)   The chord of the Diminished 7th in place of chord V is extremely useful in minor harmonisation, in any position: which notes of the C harmonic minor scale does this chord *not* contain? Explore the possibilities of all positions in harmonising the descending C harmonic minor scale, beginning:

Ex. 98a

or

(v)   You may have used a different diminished 7th chord in the contrary version of the melodic minor scale in (ii) above, when the raised 6th was accompanied by the 3rd of the scale (example 98b). That chord is in fact an inversion of the diminished 7th chord on the leading note belonging to the Dominant key (example 98c). This can be used when the 3rd of the tonic scale is in the melody.

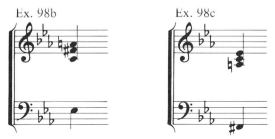

Ex. 98b   Ex. 98c

The chord of the diminished 7th can be derived from V^9 (with a *minor* 9th in a minor key) like this, in C minor:

or, as Bach uses it in Gavotte I, page 98 bar 27:

but its 'natural habitat' (or root when you think of it as VII^7) is on the leading note of a key.

(vi)   Now play your harmonisation of any major or minor scale as an accompaniment for a singer or string player, sustaining each degree of the scale. Here are three well-tried possibilities for separate keyboard accompaniment patterns:

etc.

4 Galop

Tempo di Galop

after Sullivan or Offenbach

(i)   No-one who has learnt to landscape should be disconcerted by the sight of a lot of fast-looking notes. A few slow ones may require much more ingenuity to harmonise effectively. Landscaping is vital here.

(ii)   This kind of dance is associated with the busy *frou-frou* of can-can dancers' skirts. Try to imitate a fast 'oom-pah' accompaniment of pizzicato (plucked) strings in a theatre orchestra, like this:

Sing the melody, then try to find a violinist or another instrumentalist to play it with you, or hum it yourself. How will you arrange the bass of bar 2? You may hear the right bass note but misinterpret the chord. If you are in doubt, go back to your landscape.

Using V^7, put the 7th of the chord at the top of the right hand, and maintain it for bar 3. What is then required to achieve the climax in the final bar? Observe how the bass note you probably sensed as right for bar 2 changes its role at the end of the line, where it should assert its strength.

(iii)   Common errors are:

(a)   viewing the melodic interval of the 5th in bar 2 as a root 5th, instead of asking the ear whether the harmony required at that point is major or minor,

(b)   being misled by accidentals which are merely decorative and missing the essential modulation where no accidental is visible.

You will notice that in this very common style of accompaniment the off-beat pulsation of a dominant pivot note means that the strong beat in dominant bars will be an inversion. Hence, though the 2nd degree occurs on the strong beat in the bass, to play the chord of II lets you down badly. The same problem recurs frequently, in different contexts. Pay particular attention to the importance of that 2nd-degree bass note with its two different functions in this short passage. The sequence of chords required here is revealed as extremely simple and neat. In terms of the key of C it is based on:

Ex. 101a

Ex. 101b

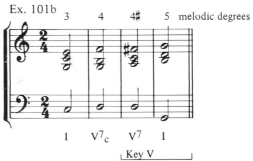

Repeat this sequence, first in 10ths then with full chords, in the key of B flat.

(iv)   Having learnt this chord progression as four chords of equal length, in B flat, match them to the Galop.

(v)   Play your accompaniment through all keys with a soloist transposing as well, by starting the sequence again, using the last chord of

225

each four bars as the first of the next four. Be careful to begin each four bars with the *right arrangement of the first chord* in the new key.

5 Waltz (Tschaikowsky)

from The Sleeping Beauty

(i)   It is as important not to be deceived by the apparent length and 'slow' notation of pieces like this waltz as not to be put off by the welter of notes in the melody of the Galop and other pieces of its kind. The historical progress from the stately Minuet, with its clear three beats and changes of harmony within the bar, to the 19th-century Scherzo and Waltz (still conventionally written in $\frac{3}{4}$ time even when $\frac{6}{8}$, $\frac{9}{8}$ or $\frac{12}{8}$ might seem more appropriate) requires the interpreter to recognise that *bars* should be regarded as *beats*, from the harmonic as well as the rhythmic point of view. It will be found that increasing richness of harmonic detail often lies over surprisingly sparse landscaping. You can prove this for yourself by landscaping this waltz in two ways:

(a)   Landscape with a change of 5th per bar.
(b)   Landscape with a change of 5th per four-bar unit, except where you feel a faster change of pace to be essential.

Which version comes nearer to your memory of the original waltz?

(ii)   In providing the harmonic framework, the more convincing landscape will also reveal the many bars and first beats which constitute melodic passing notes and appoggiaturas, without which you would be unable to render this piece to your satisfaction, whether or not you choose exactly the same harmonies as Tschaikovsky. Compare (a) and (b):

Ex. 102a

Ex. 102b

Having landscaped the piece, you will understand that in example 102b, bar 2 is *not* chord III$_b$, but I$_c$ with the melody note a passing note under the tonic, to which it will return (as in bar 4) because it is part of a four-bar tonic unit. (This situation frequently occurs in 19th-century piano music and *lieder* accompaniments.) Four introductory bars before the entry of the melody should similarly alternate between I and I$_c$, not I and V. Continue to incorporate the 'pah-pahs' beneath the melody with your right hand. Only in slow waltzes is it usually practicable to play them with a jumping left hand.

(iii)   Provide dominant bars with a similar alternation in the bass between root position and 1st or 2nd inversion, the right hand supplying the 'pah-pahs' with the close 'two-note' pair, or whichever two notes of the chord combine easily with the melody.

(iv)   Bars 9 to 12 may be treated by $\frac{}{3}$, which you should first play in single solid chords, *omitting bar 10*. Then slot in bar 10 by parallel chromatic $\frac{}{3}$ and you will probably hear how to fill in the rest of that chord. If in doubt, play the passage in three parts only and note the importance of the $e^{b\prime}$ binding-note. Then name the chord.

   Alternatively, you can treat the bass in contrary motion, by scalic ascent from the landscaping chord V.

(v)   Your landscaping may have suggested the same or different treatment for melody bars 5 to 8, when they are repeated as bars 21 to 24.

(vi)   Bars 25–26 are difficult. When landscaping, you would be wise to leave such an area un-sketched, until you have settled the cadential harmonies of the final bars. Then, as with a jigsaw puzzle, work backwards to fill the gap. The whole section can be handled on a dominant pedal bass of the final key; but it is worth experimenting with a moving bass for this section.

(vii) Finally, to bring your setting closer to Tschaikovsky's, play the melody in the *middle* of the texture. Keep it singing sonorously with the lower fingers of the right hand, adding light 'pah-pahs' above it. This will sound best in the key of B flat, beginning:

Ex. 102c

Notice that in bar 3 a single 'pah' is adequate.

Students taught from the outset to do detailed harmonisations of short passages, instead of sketching complete pieces as advocated here, and who are allowed to use many chords and inversions before they really understand tonality, are inclined to confuse the word 'primary' with the idea of 'preliminary'. So arises the tacit assumption that, as you progress, you should put away childish things and make substantial, even predominant, use of secondary chords. But 'primary' in this connection has nothing to do with educational grading. The description 'primary chords' means that those chords are of *prime importance*. No enlargement of harmonic vocabulary will alter that fact, for it is rooted in the science of sound. Study of the bulk of composed music provides overwhelming evidence of this, from Bach to Stravinsky.

Some contemporary composers, who appear to ignore the basic acoustic system, either take the lower areas of the harmonic series for granted and use the upper areas only—as we have seen, the series rises into smaller and smaller intervals, called 'microtones'—or intentionally seek new effects through the contradiction of natural acoustics, a contradiction that can only be made in the light of the thing that is contradicted.

Finally, you are recommended to go through all the chapters again, which will establish more thoroughly what you have learnt and should encourage you by the greater ease and speed with which you are able to replay the pieces. If you can, play all the melodies as well as their harmonisations by memory—by ear. At the same time, use additional melodies from any books which do *not* provide chord symbols. Other melodies will not, of course, be grouped together for their suitability to particular treatments, as in these chapters: you will have to decide entirely for yourself what treatments are suitable. It is then useful to make a list of pieces you can play by ear. Professional or amateur, you will find yourself with a never-ending challenge and source of musical enjoyment . . . in sketching at the keyboard.

USEFUL SOURCES FOR HARMONISING MELODIES

These books were all in print when this book was published and should be obtainable from music dealers or bookshops. In case of difficulty, the publishers will usually accept orders at the following addresses:

Oxford University Press, Saxon Way West, Corby, Northamptonshire.
English Folk Dance and Song Society, Cecil Sharp House, 2 Regents
    Park Road, London NW1 7AY

O.U.P.:
Appleby and C, *Sing Together*. Melody Edition. 0 19 330155 5.
Crowe and C, *Folk Song Sight Singing*, Book 1 (0 19 330251 9);
    Book 2 (0 19 330252 7); Book 3 (0 19 330253 5); Book 4 (19 330254 3);
    Book 5 (0 19 330255 1); Book 6 (0 19 330256 X); Book 7 (0 19 330257 8).
Vaughan Williams and C, *The Oxford Book of Carols for Schools*.
    Melody Edition. 0 19 330831 2.
Wiseman and C, *The Clarendon Book of Carols*, Book 2. Melody Edition.
    0 19 330773 1.
Wiseman and C, *The Clarendon Book of Unison Songs for Juniors*.
Melody Edition. 0 19 330801 0.

E.F.D.S.S.:
Any melody edition from Catalogue No. 1 (Folk Dance Books), or from
Catalogue No. 2 (Folk Song Books).

It is essential to use melody editions without added chord symbols. Many of these may also be found in Recorder Tutors.

APPENDIX AND NOTES FOR TEACHERS

Some of these notes are intended for class and individual teachers as follow-up material. Some are suggested 'answers'. DO NOT look at these suggestions until after you have made your own solutions to the pieces concerned, as this curbs your experiments, through which you learn and your critical judgement develops.

1 Three Blind Mice

(a)

This usual first attempt at the third phrase is dull, because it is insufficiently differentiated from the twofold phrases, and the final single phrase is not brought into relief.

Restriction to playing and harmonising always in the middle of the keyboard breeds timidity in the use of extreme registers. Encouragement is needed to play:

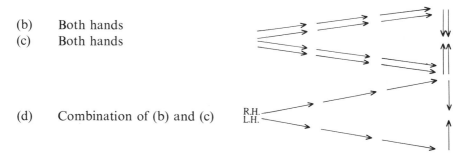

(b)   Both hands

(c)   Both hands

(d)   Combination of (b) and (c)

This could also be reversed; but divergence better reinforces crescendo, tying up with mounting dramatic tension.

2 Come Home Now

Verbal repetition calls for differentiation: therefore the first four bars constitute three phrases: short, short, long.

Interpreted as 'light, light, strong', suitable registration becomes 'solo, solo, doubled'. To start R.H. and drop to L.H. for the repeat of the first bar integrates better than raising the register. To alter the registration on the repeat of these four bars would confuse rather than clarify.

Bars 9–12 provide a very weak contrast melodically; but this can be strengthened by registration in contrary directions, R.H. up and L.H. down. Maintain this throughout the four bars, to avoid the fiddliness of more short phrases. Recapitulation as before. Playing by memory reveals that remembering the notes is little problem, once the form of the piece is highlighted in this way.

3 Hot Cross Buns

The usual attempt at the third phrase is:

No teacher's comment is needed for a pupil to hear that this is unsatisfactory. Play the melody from *d″* down to *g′* with the right hand. Invert it with the same hand, then transfer the inversion to the left hand and play both hands together, linking with the ending. Why was the first attempt unsatisfactory? The answer lies in the horizontal nature of harmony as expressed by a melody, which can be illustrated so:

= G chord

= D chord

Therefore both hands need to run up and down the *same* chord:

G chord

G chord

4 Captain Morgan's March

CHORUS, *second time*

232

5 Papa a du Tabac

This is one suggestion for registration, but it should not be regarded as an obligatory pattern:

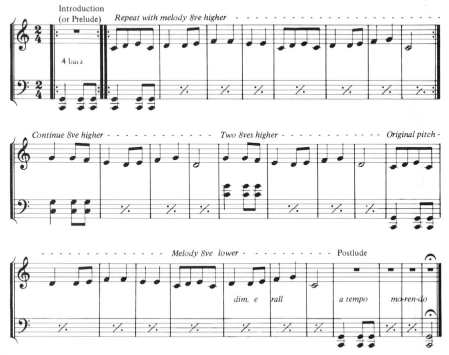

6 Patapan

The two suggested rhythms are  or . The sparser accompaniment enables the melody to flow faster.

7 Skip to my Lou

This series of sketches shows the search for a rhythm that establishes the correct pace of a song:

(a)

This accompanimental rhythm overweights the melody and slows it down.

(b)

This gains *élan* from the omission of the 2nd beat, but its mere metre makes no contribution.

(c)

This turns out to be the first rhythm played twice as slow, so that it speeds the pace; but it sits down on the end of each phrase.

(d)

The replacement of the (a) figure for bar 2 links phrases, but is still somewhat fussy and heavy.

(e)

A mere tie now produces the ideal ground rhythm, propelling the piece light-footedly forward from phrase to phrase.

This process has revealed that, as there can be strong and weak beats, so there can also be strong and weak bars. The difference between bars and beats is not absolute, but depends on the choice of the writer. To establish the pace of a melody is to find the reality of its rhythmic nature, independent of notational idiosyncrasies.

8 This Old Man

Compare these four bass rhythms: (a)|♫ ♩| (b)|♩ ♩| (c)|♩ ♫| (d)|♩. ♪|

9 Spring Song

10 Further Variations

Suggested rhythmic accompanimental patterns for these five songs are indicated below by single notes only, to represent the pair of notes (keynote plus 5th above). Tails down indicate that the interval of a 5th should be played by the left hand, tails up that it should be played by the right hand (when the melody is being sung).

Spring Song: ³⁄₄ ♩. or ³⁄₄ ♩ ♩ or ³⁄₄ ♩. |♩.|

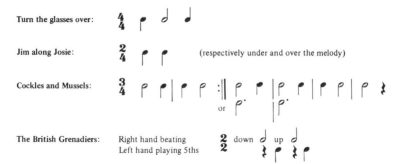

Turn the glasses over:

Jim along Josie: (respectively under and over the melody)

Cockles and Mussels:

The British Grenadiers: Right hand beating
Left hand playing 5ths

11 Girls and boys come out to play (Verse 2)

12 Green and White

To introduce a beginner to any two chords in this form:

is equivalent to expecting someone to learn to swim in a puddle! He or she needs a swimming bath—to be able to do a 'length' of one harmony and a 'length' of another, as suggested in 'Girls and boys come out to play'. By the time this song is reached, the pace is fining down to a 'stroke' of each.

Bar 1: Beneath the root of a chord, close register will always sound very bare. Low register is best here, as it leaves room for the 3rd of the chord (10th above the root) to be generated as an overtone of the bass 5th.

B.2–4: A repeated chord weakens bar 3 (second strongest bar in a 4-bar phrase). This registration is equivalent to the strong 'HXB' bass.

B.9–12: Close register is perfect in bar 9, because the 3rd of the chord is in the melody. As there are two 2-bar phrases here, and contrast is an asset in this slightly differentiated section, the two Dominant 5ths may effectively remain in the same register.

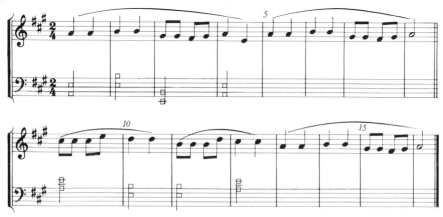

235

13 Andulko

An interesting experiment may be made if beginners landscape this song entirely with I and V, whilst more experienced pupils are encouraged to harmonise it quite freely. The whole character of the song surely indicates a one-in-a-bar pace. Much heavy weather may be made with note-for-note harmonisations; but instruction to use chords I and V only, with one 5th per bar, quickly produces:

Nor is this only beginners' stuff: it provides the framework for the following lively pianistic arrangement, in which only one extra harmony is used (optionally):

There is no need for a lot of mystique to surround the multiple dominants (V^9, V^{11} and V^{13}) which, together with accented passing notes (which the former *are*) and 'suspensions' have unnecessarily been reserved solely for advanced harmony students, despite the presence of these features in the folk music of peasants, sailors and children, none of them versed in harmonic theory. Sparse harmonisation makes possible their early introduction and enables students to experience the *feel* of these devices (for they are profoundly linked with rhythmic stress and flow) and to understand them very clearly, so facilitating later work.

The beginner who felt that the Dominant 5th sounded right under bar 5 of 'Andulko' would be using V^9, with no need to name it. The following diagram shows the series, in terms of the Dominant of the key of C:

236

The *a'* in bar 5 of 'Andulko' can equally be viewed as an accented passing note, which falls onto the Dominant note itself.

Study of the harmonic series shows what the honest ear must observe, that the extent to which sounds prove mellifluous or jarring depends not so much on *what* they are as on *where* they are, in relation to each other. In the second bar listen to the effect on the D when the low C is subsequently sounded:

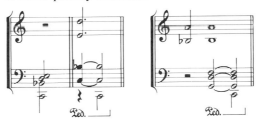

Here is a chord from Delius's Serenade (*Hassan*), nine bars before the end, which looks as though it will be far more discordant than it proves in the sounding:

Play an octave *Bb,,* beneath it and it is hardly so at all; for it is perfectly arranged according to the harmonic series, the *a♭-a♮* corresponding to the *b♭''* in the third octave and *b♮''* in the fourth octave of the frontispiece diagram (page vi).

As the series contains all sounds in due course, a discord can be described as 'an assemblage of sounds, deprived of sufficient sub-structure to define them as upper partials of a single fundamental'. As has been explained, the placing of the major 3rd within the root and 5th at a low register, and especially the doubling of that 3rd in the octave above, causes confusion by a mixture of fundamentals.

It may be of interest to note that, above the fourth octave of the series, the intervals become semitones and less. This structure of the harmonic series no doubt explains the special capacity of a 'Dominant Pedal' to carry a rich kaleidoscope of chromaticisms, building to a climax of tension before relaxing into the final cadence of a fugue—the musical form in which Dominant Pedals are a special feature.

This and another song with prominent V⁹, 'John Smith', appear in Chapter 9. It is however, a feature of many simple melodies based on Tonic and Dominant harmonies that they may contain no 6th degree of the scale.

14 In dulci jubilo

Why does registration make a difference? Play the two 5ths simultaneously, and they will both be heard as part of the same series (based on a lower 5th, C-G, with the fundamental an octave below that):

This succession seems to remove the brash effect of two neighbouring harmonic series. Nevertheless, the character of chord IV, struck, is totally different from the character of V^7, V^9, V^{11}.

If, through the process of harmonic landscaping, you learn to choose the right chords you will infrequently come up against the problem of parallels, except in the case of IV-V. But this is a particularly bad sounding one. Why? Remove the 5ths and use only single adjacent bass notes under "Alpha es et" in bar 13. Is that better?

To many ears the objectionable parallelism between chords IV and V, especially in a major key, is detectable even when the 5ths are missing. It seems indeed that the inner 'tritone' (four notes with three whole tones between them) delineated by these notes may be the principal cause of offence:

Tritone

In mediaeval times the tritone was known as *Diabolus in Musica* ('The devil in music'). It proves useful to be able to hear within such 10ths the indication of parallel neighbouring chords.

15 Sacramento

(a) Though reasonable to start with one Tonic 5th per bar, it will soon be recognised that a crotchet pace is better, in order to point the syncopation in bars 3–4.

Though adherence to Tonic throughout is normally expected to yield little other than rhythmic landscaping, it also makes a harmonic contribution here; for the chord of I proves satisfactory under the 6th degree of the scale in bar 2. Still more important, the Tonic chord is essential at the commencement of the final bar, producing a suspension. And the indication of *when* the harmonies must occur in the last two bars is vital to the sense of this piece.

(b) Sketched in Primary 5ths, a version on the following lines should be produced with comparative ease, suspensions and anticipations handled with near professional competence at this early stage of study:

238

To clarify these special features, a diagonal line slanting to the right from bass chord to delayed melody note indicates that an accented passing-note, appoggiatura or suspension has sounded at the rhythmic moment when the chord was struck. Conversely, when the line slants to the right from melody note to bass chord this indicates 'anticipation', the melody note having tripped forward in advance of the chord of which it forms a part. Look again at the Mendelssohn variation quoted on page 36 which is full of anticipations, appoggiaturas and suspensions.

The identical melody in bars 2 and 6 is illustrated with two alternatives.

16 Primary Chords

The complete diagram should read:

In any key, the primary chords will be I, V and IV. It will be seen that the upper row of chords shows harmonisation by I and V only.

17 The Advantages of Landscaping

By contrast, the player using single notes (or varying intervals) in the bass by no means necessarily knows what chord he is using, or what degree of that chord his bass note is—root, 3rd, 5th or 7th. So the character of a chord may pass by unrecognised by the player. For whereas a 5th inevitably prescribes a root position of the chord on its bottom note, a single bass note could be a part of many chords

In terms of the concern of this chapter with bass notes on the 4th and 5th degrees of the scale, these two degrees might carry chords IV and V, or they might carry chords that would be labelled II_b-I_c: the former situation open to problems, the latter not. If you use 5ths you can be virtually certain they are IV and V.

239

18 The Drunken Sailor

Study the following alternatives:

Chapter 11 begins with an accompaniment for this song.

19 The Tailor and the Mouse

Preliminary landscaping of I, V, V, I, is adequate for the first phrase; but the two adjacent bars of V are rather weak. In which bar is it more important to retain V? Obviously bar 3, because of its cadential function. Is there an alternative chord for bar 2? Notice that no 3rd of the chord is necessary in bar 3, as the sound evoked is obviously minor in the context.

After completing the song, students should compare their choice of harmonies with those in the following 19th-century arrangement:

Discussion of alternatives nurtures sensitivity to style. Students who might previously have taken any printed edition as gospel are now likely to remark upon bars 11–12 above, some admiring the treatment, others considering it out of style. The melody contains no 6th degree and student arrangements are likely to be VII for both bars, or VII-II:

postulating Dorian. The above arrangement has assumed a diatonic minor key signature (or Aeolian) and used a 19th-century idiom at this point.

20 Greensleeves

241

The British Broadside Ballad and its Music, Claude Simpson (New Brunswick) investigates the history of this melody and illustrates many variants.

The path of fashion in history may sometimes be likened to clouds crossing the moon, as is revealed by the following far-sighted paragraph by Dr. W. Pole in 1879, quoted in the article on 'Modes' in *The Oxford Companion to Music*:

> It is by no means impossible that composers of genius might some day open for themselves a considerable field for novelty and originality by shaking off the trammels of our restricted modern tonality; and that they might find scope for the development of the art in some kind of return to the principles of the ancient forms [of the scale] which at present are only looked down upon as remnants of a barbarous age.

How right was his prophecy, made in the year when Vaughan Williams was seven years old, Holst five, and Bartok yet unborn. But a century later the teaching of basic harmony is still almost solely concerned with that 'restricted modern tonality', despite the fact that the majority of minor folk songs are not diatonic minors at all but are emphatically modal.

21 The Oak and the Ash

Either I, V, I, V or I, VII, I, V. Does chord V in bar 2 suggest a minor or major chord? In bar 4 it is defined as major (the $b^{\natural\prime}$ is only a semitone lower mordent).

22 The Animals Went in Two by Two

Which is preferable, the same harmony for bars 3–4 and 7–8, or different? It is in the next six bars that careful listening is essential to diagnose the harmonic implications of the melody. For the unconsidered playing of 5ths that will 'fit' (on G, C, G, D) will prevent discovery of the musical logic at this point. Registration is also important, for even the playing of this may be followed by hesitation:

Whereas if the B♭ 5th is raised, so as to *drop* to the F 5th, the two chords will interrelate, and treatment of the ensuing sequential bars becomes obvious.

Yet "all went into the ark" can still go astray, unless the melodic connection between these two bars and the preceding four is recognised. This musical device is called 'rhythmic diminution'. It is a common developmental device in sophisticated musical forms, especially fugue, as is also 'rhythmic augmentation' in which the note values are lengthened. This grouping together of modal chords III and VII, followed sequentially by I and V, makes III and VII sound like Tonic and Dominant of the 'relative major' key. So this example indicates how the diatonic system began to evolve out of the modal.

The bass (minor chords shown in small notes) for the whole is:

Students should thoroughly familiarise themselves with this piece and play it also in the modes on A and E. The following diagram, applicable to both Dorian and Aeolian Modes (as none of the chords contains any 6th degree of the scale) may prove useful:

23 Belle Qui Tiens Ma Vie (Pavane)

Students should compare their own versions with the following setting in 5ths (to be played in ♩ ♫ rhythm throughout) and with the two arrangements:

243

The cadential bars reveal the origin of what is now called the 'cadential 2nd inversion' of chord I as being simply an appoggiatura (accented passing note) over chord V:

bb. 27-28

bb. 11-12

Both have a single appoggiatura which causes a discordant 7th between the top and middle notes. Later versions of this cadence acquired a *double* appoggiatura, which erased the discordant 7th:

and as late as 1800 it was common to write this cadence as a double appoggiatura, especially in:

played

I$_c$ V   I

In 1588 a monk known as Thoinot Arbeau published *Orchésographie* in which he described the court dances of the period in the form of lessons to an imaginary young aristocrat named Capriol. He gives this Pavane in the following choral arrangement. It was from this volume that Peter Warlock drew the material for his *Capriol* Suite, from which a piano arrangement of the Pavane is shown below. Harmonic landscaping may be seen as a common denominator between the two settings. It may also be appreciated how the ability to sense the skeleton of a piece in this way can help the sight-reader or arranger to judge what is essential and what may be omitted.

Version in *Orchesographie* by Arbeau

Adapted from *Capriol Suite* by Warlock

24 Charlie is my Darling

At this stage in the work it can be very salutary for the teacher to play the melody of
'Charlie is my Darling' for pupils to take down from dictation, so linking what they
have been learning with pitch aural tests. Some important points to remember can be
brought home in this way. Owing to the conventional formula of musical dictation
tests, pupils expect to be told the key of a piece. In this case it is wise to give only the key
signature of three flats, whereupon some will start on $e^{b\prime}$ and not realise the tonality of
what they have written, which should be played to them. This is much more valuable
than simply being marked 'right' or 'wrong'. Even when the correct key is established

versions of the middle section are sure to include:

These, too, should be played back to their writers, so they may make their own corrections. The unfortunate dominance of the harmonic minor scale in instrumental teaching leaves many students insufficiently aware that the 6th as well as the 7th degree may need raising.

It is not uncommon for students to say that bar 5 has "gone into G", which suggests that they would use a D major chord on the 2nd beat. This is the sort of nonsense that can so easily be written when a one-beat harmonic pace is permitted before the harmonic structuring of a total phrase has been understood.

In bar 7, if you keep to modal thinking, the two chords will be VI and III, but the effect on diatonic ears is of a passing change to IV-I in the 'relative major' before returning to the Imperfect Cadence in bar 8. What kind of 'B' is necessary (or desirable) in the G 5th of bar 8? Remind yourself of the value of example 30 on page 80.

25 The Miller of Dee

Diatonic treatment:

Notice how this registration provides drive and gives accent to the 3rd bar; but other patterns are also possible. If you treat the tune modally, note that there is no fixed 6th degree (E) to put in the signature and that the 7th degree is raised in bars 1 and 3 but *not* in bar 2:

26 Czech Folk Tune

Those who do not listen with a 'diagnostic' ear to the harmonic implications of the melody may still miss the logic of the first section. The remedy is to landscape with only one 5th per phrase.

Do the same with the two-bar phrases. Then decide the type of cadence, so determining the second bar chord—the placing of which will be found to highlight the phrasing. Should the discord be felt excessive, simply maintain the top note of the first 5th and play only the bottom note of the second one. The relationship with bar 12 of 'The Miller of Dee' will then be evident: no further thickening is needed here.

Students who harmonise bar 3 as follows should be led to find their own correction through being asked to treat this progression sequentially in the ensuing four bars. This will be found impossible.

Attention should then be drawn to the fact that in the modal 'The Oak and the Ash' (page 81) the following three alternatives were all valid:

But when modal melodies become more organised formally and contain phrases repeated in sequence, the chord of VII ceases to be usable in tonic minor areas and now only functions as dominant of the relative major key (as in bars 7 and 10 of this Czech melody). This comparison illustrates a principal difference between modal and diatonic minor music.

27 Bourrée

Bar 2 can be landscaped with only one 5th, but is better with two. The same sequence should be recapitulated within the penultimate bar. Bars 3–4 with one 5th per bar, I–III, is too modal for this piece: an additional 5th is needed to smooth the path, in fact to effect a modulation, ready for the central section. It will fall on the fourth beat.

Seemingly equally valid at bar 4, and adequately landscaped with one 5th per bar, is an Imperfect Cadence in the tonic key. Students should be asked to sing the 3rd they imagine present in the final chord. (See example 29b.) This cadence, too, may have an additional harmony on the last beat of bar 3. But the right-sounding chord will be heard to produce glaring parallel 5ths with the melody. Chord VI may be preferred by some, for good reason, but is in fact a decoy! The problem will be dealt with in the next dance. In any case, the Imperfect Cadence is the less suitable here, in the light of the next phrase.

28 Gavotte

The setting of this piece as an entrance test for first-study musicians in a college of education revealed candidate after candidate ruining the rhythm, by harmonising every crotchet beat including the anacrusis with solid chords of uniform weight, then upsetting the tonality by missing the sequence in the relative major key and carrying on oblivious in the minor—the occasional student recognising by the end of the phrase that he was off the rails! There could be no better proof of the need for teaching harmonic landscaping.

The bass should be:

For those who have already used inversions (See Chapter 8, page 111.)

Bars 3–4 bring a problem of avoiding parallels (see Chapter 4). Restricted to 5ths, the only way to avoid parallels is to use I alone in bar 3. But IV is needed (if included in the identical first bar) so that, as landscaping, the sequence is correct. The solution to parallel IV-V is to invert one of the chords. In this case use chord IV in 1st inversion (*i.e.* with the 3rd of the chord at the bottom) so that the bass moves in contrary motion to the melody:

Landscaping: Detailing:

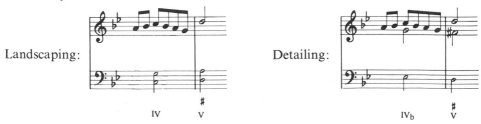

IV   V   IVb   V

Students may be asked to apply this treatment to the second phrase of the foregoing Bourrée. It will now be clear that anyone who chose to precede chord V by chord VI was hearing the ideal *bass* note in the context; but the chord in question requires to be a minor inversion, not a major root position.

29 Mattachins

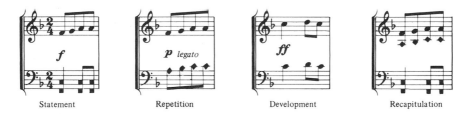

| Statement | Repetition | Development | Recapitulation |

30 Transposing Modulation

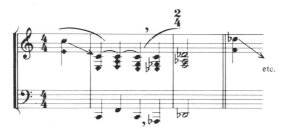

31 Rock-a-bye Baby

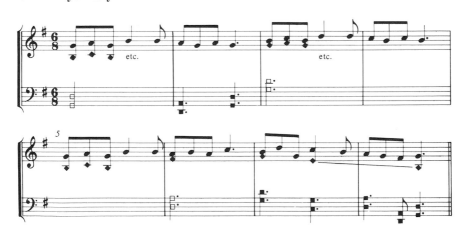

32 Joys Seven

This technique is particularly useful for any music teacher and accompanist, since it applies to the accompaniment of instrumental playing as well as to singing. Not only will soloists or groups sing and play much better when the melodic line is *not* doubled by the piano, but the teacher can hear the melody much better and can detect more easily such faults as bad intonation, late entries or poor phrasing. There is also an added incentive for singers and players when they feel that they alone are responsible for a melody line. Always to play the melody line in a piano accompaniment encourages laziness. The extreme economy of this process is a further asset in that it provides a minimal accompaniment of great clarity, which nevertheless gives both harmonic and rhythmic support. Too many 'easy' arrangements for the unskilled consist of occasional chords, of hymnal thickness, and provide no rhythmic contribution. Any young teacher who is an elementary pianist will be in better control of a class when attention that might otherwise be focussed on the score can be given to the class.

33 Minuet (Beethoven)

34 Sacramento

250

Appoggiaturas, anticipations and suspensions in the landscaping become 'in step' with a typical plucked-string syncopated accompaniment, because the single bass note is common to *both* melody notes in the pair and the defining 6th is concordant with the off-beat melody note. Chord IV in bar 6 is discarded in favour of I and will now be used only in the chorus.

35 What shall we do with the Drunken Sailor?

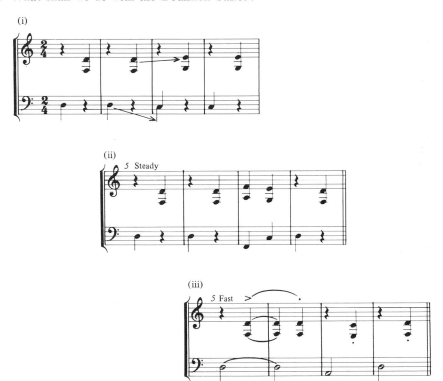

36 The Animals Went in Two by Two

Bars 9 to 12 form a sequence of chords common in much modal music and it is important to use the 'right' 6th—stylistically—above the bass:

(note that in bars 13-14 right and left hands will coincide)

If you choose to play 6ths a 3rd higher, doubling the tune, you will find yourself using V^7 chords which will be out of place here but quite appropriate, say, to a piece in the style of Schubert:

The advantage of playing only 6ths with the right hand in the song passage may be revealed by the more ambitious; for a three-note chord containing a wrong middle note will alter the harmony and the thicker texture is not necessarily an improvement.

37 Nonesuch

38 Czech Folk Tune

If you have already followed Chapter 8 you may remember that the importance to formal structure of the Interrupted Cadence was studied in connection with the extended phrasing of 'Upon Paul's Steeple'. There, in a major context, the chord of VI was minor. Hence the surprise, when a major chord (perfect cadence) had been expected. In America it is known as an 'unexpected' or 'surprise cadence'. Here we meet the equivalent situation in minor music, where the chord of VI is contrastingly major. It postpones the return to the key chord. Landscaping of the second line should now stand:

The move from VI to I can also be improved and the home bass note of F still further delayed. Allow a departure from 5ths in favour of a single bass note, indicating an inversion of the Tonic chord. Either a cadential second inversion or a first inversion would be good here. Which do you prefer?

If the first inversion is chosen, it may be linked by a passing note, on the last quaver of bar 14, to move stepwise up to the Dominant bass in the cadential bar.

39 Gavotte

To derive a contrapuntal accompaniment from landscaping:

Notice how parallel IV-V, in bars 3–4 in the landscaping stage, is avoided in the finished counterpoint (see the Appendix, page 248).

253

40 The Chord on the 7th Degree

Though each scale contains seven melodic degrees, only six of their triads comprise perfect 5ths. The remaining seventh note (leading note in major tonality, 2nd degree in diatonic minor tonality) carries a diminished 5th; and, as can be seen in the harmonic series, a diminished triad (e'-g'-$b^{b'}$ there, b-d'-f' here) is the upper portion of a chord whose root and 5th *are* a perfect 5th apart:

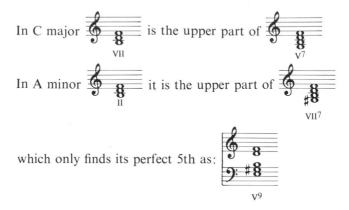

which only finds its perfect 5th as:

41 Secondary Chords

In modal and minor harmonisation both kinds of chords, major and minor, have essentially been used in landscaping. Secondary—minor—chords have a different function in major tonality, and are very rarely used in landscaping; they are generally better introduced, as second thoughts, if you want to vary the texture. One exception is, occasionally, chord VI. In the previous chapter, this chord was used in the second landscaping of the Czech melody in F minor, at the beginning of the final recapitulatory phrase. But this *was* a second sketch: and chord VI, on d^{b}, was introduced as an alternative to chord I. The whole effect of an Interrupted Cadence (to which this choice was allied) is that the chord of VI occurs where chord I was expected, so it is heard by the listener in the light of an alternative chord.

42 This Old Man   *Numbers refer to Chapter 14.*

1(ii) Though a process studied in Chapter 2, choice of a suitable Tonic 5th drone bass still seems to produce problems. Suggested rhythms usually include (a) ♫ ♩ (b) ♩ ♫ and (c) ♩ ♫ .

    (a)   is coarse and heavy and contributes nothing, merely doubling the melody and impeding its flow.

    (b)   meets with more approval, yet is still somewhat heavy. What aspect of this rhythm is an advantage over the first? Once that question is answered the clue is provided for

    (c)   which amounts to ♩. ♪. Even at this stage some students have difficulty in maintaining this rhythmic counterpoint throughout.

With regard to (a), identity of accompanimental rhythm with *melodic* rhythmic pattern is rarely ideal if the accompaniment is detached in character from the melody. When a melody is harmonised at the pace of its component notes, as later in this chapter, the situation is different; because the notes sung or played beneath it, though they should provide logical horizontal lines, become amalgamated with the melody in a way that a detached rhythmic accompaniment cannot and should not. Registration plays a principal part in achieving amalgamation or detachment, as has been emphasised from the outset of Part I. Reference to the harmonic series explains why this is so.

1(iii) An essential element of style is consistency. Consistency carries conviction (which can include consistent use of the apparently inconsistent!). The pace of harmonic change when this melody is landscaped by primary 5ths involves a final cadence between bar and bar:

not between beat and beat within the last bar. That faster pace will be found consistent with a subsequent sketch process.

1(ix) The problem arises if a *d'* has been played in the middle as thumb-note on the third quaver. It may be the minor chord that *d'* produces which sounds wrong, or the resulting parallel progression between third and fourth quaver beats. Both situations lead to a confusion of tonality (see the first part of Chapter 12), for after the G minor chord it would seem quite logical to continue:

Placing chord II next to chord I in this manner is not a good plan in a major context, as it suggests chords I and VII in modal tonality (see Chapter 5). The chord required on that third quaver is the second inversion of the dominant 7th (V^7_c), the thumb-note preferably *c'*, but could be *e'*. The use of chord II in place of V_c is a very common mistake, frequently made by students who do hear the right bass note, but do not pay sufficient aural attention to the *quality* of chord—major or minor—that the 2nd-degree bass note has to carry. The fault is still more liable to be made beneath a 4th-degree melody note, when degrees 4 and 2 are both calculated (theoretically) to belong to chord II and it is forgotten that the interval of a 3rd which they comprise is also the top 3rd of the chord of V^7, a chord which contains *three* thirds (see page 105).

1(xi) Analysis of the chords produced as a by-product of the horizontal process will reveal, after the alternations of I and I_b, IV-I_b-V^7_c-I-V_b-I-V^7_c. The essence of music, even four-part harmony, is to progress horizontally. Support for this natural musical way to learn harmony, gradually enriching a horizontal structure from within, may be found in the following:

3rds Bass ($\frac{}{3}$): I_b I I_b | I_b I I_b | IV I_b V^7_c I | V_b I V^7_c |

Landscaping: I............. | I............. | IV................. | V.............. |

43 Down in Demerara

44 Leave her, Johnny

(a)   Phrase 1: $\frac{3}{5}$.   2: $\frac{}{3}$.   3: $\frac{}{3}$.   4: $\frac{6}{}$.

(b) $\begin{array}{c}2\\4\end{array}$ I | I | V_b | I I_b | IV | I_b I | I_b I V_b VI | I_c V | I

(c)

Notice how the horizontal processes are obscured in normal notation. This is why different shapes are used to illustrate the way in which players should *think* in order to achieve the horizontal flow so essential to music. There is no need to use any notational devices as the processes are learnt in action. But in the few cases where writing *has* been recommended (as in the charts of chords in Chapters 4, 5 and 6) it may be useful to write notes in different shapes (or colours as on the front cover) to help memory.

Do not write anything on melodies in printed songbooks other than phrase marks,

256

because it is essential that your ear should continue to be the guide on repeat performances. If there are visual indications of procedure, the eye will inevitably take over from the ear. Lack of written symbols also leaves the field open for varying interpretations and difficult passages have to be re-thought: this is the best way to find final solutions, since first thoughts are not always necessarily the best.

Shorthand signs can also be useful for taking notes or collecting further material for suitable treatment, the signs written under piece titles, not melody areas.

Analysis of individual chords is necessary for the serious student at some stage, but should follow playing not precede it—sound before symbol. So harmony becomes *experienced* in its own terms of sound, before notational symbols are introduced. This approach leads to chance discovery of sounds that you might not have considered from visual analysis alone. Nevertheless, you must always use judgement to assess which sounds are relevant in a given context and style. Indulgent 'free-for-all' does not teach anyone anything. Be chary of new elements before you are ready to incorporate them, one concept at a time. Free improvisation or composition is another matter and you will doubtless find notation essential when you compose your own pieces. But do not encourage yourself (or fond parents) to think that writing notes is necessarily composing.

45 The Bells of Aberdovey

Try $\frac{3}{5}$ with descending registration of 5ths on beats 1 and 4. Verbal counts specify quaver pace. What is the appropriate cadence to end bar 3? An alternative to $\frac{}{3}$ may be worked out vertically over a scalic bass.

46 Captain Morgan's March

Section A: 8ves.   B: $\frac{}{3}$ plus Dominant pivot in the bass on off-beats.
C: 'inversion' sparsely filled in.

47 French Folk Song

In the close 3rds of example 89a, the 4th degree of the tonic key is raised to become leading note of the dominant key on the 2nd beat in bar 8. In example 89b, the modified degree is not present, only implied on the 2nd beat in bar 8. In example 89c, contrary $\frac{}{3}$ brings in that raised 4th on the last beat of bar 7. In example 89d, full four-part harmony, with bar 7 treated by $\frac{}{3}$, introduces the raised 4th as middle right-hand note ('alto' part) also on the last beat of bar 7.

48 All Through the Night

A d' suffices up to the last two cadential notes, but involves excessive dominant harmony and is very dull in a section which needs increased interest in comparison with the first section and its recapitulation. An e' establishes a good tonal contrast and contains more varied possibilities as the passage progresses.

49 Baa, Baa, Black Sheep (Quand Trois Poules)

Though so similar in appearance, the functions of the second and third *pairs* of bars are quite different: hence the advisability of commencing by structuring processes. The second pair demands cadential treatment but the third pair needs to convey a floating sense of onwardness, for which $\frac{1}{3}$ is ideal. It is important to get the correct chord and position of that chord in the second half of bar 1: $\frac{1}{3}$ carelessly filled in can change the implied harmony.